Foundations of Museum Studies

Foundations of
Museum Studies

Evolving Systems of Knowledge

KIERSTEN F. LATHAM
and JOHN E. SIMMONS

 **LIBRARIES UNLIMITED**

AN IMPRINT OF ABC-CLIO, LLC
Santa Barbara, California • Denver, Colorado • Oxford, England

Library of Congress Cataloging-in-Publication Data

Latham, Kiersten Foursh.
  Foundations of museum studies : evolving systems of knowledge / Kiersten F. Latham and John E. Simmons.
      pages   cm.
  Includes bibliographical references and index.
  ISBN 978-1-61069-282-3 (pbk : alk. paper) — ISBN 978-1-61069-952-5 (ebook)
1. Museums. 2. Museum techniques. 3. Museums—United States. 4. Museum techniques—United States. I. Simmons, John E. II. Title.
  AM5. L38 2014
  069—dc23   2014016908

ISBN   978-1-61069-282-3
EISBN: 978-1-61069-952-5

18   17   16   15   14   1   2   3   4   5

This book is also available on the World Wide Web as an eBook.
Visit www.abc-clio.com for details.

Libraries Unlimited
An Imprint of ABC-CLIO, LLC

ABC-CLIO, LLC
130 Cremona Drive, P.O. Box 1911
Santa Barbara, California 93116-1911

This book is printed on acid-free paper ♾
Manufactured in the United States of America

We dedicate this book to the memory of our former museum studies professor and advisor, scientist, curator, and museum director, Philip Strong Humphrey (1926–2009), who conveyed his passion and vision of museums to several generations of grateful students and colleagues.

Contents

Illustrations

Figures

Tables

Foreword

Since the expansion of academic programs began in the 1970s, museum studies has become a rapidly evolving field. Prospective museum studies students are now faced with a bewilderingly diverse array of master's degree and graduate certificate programs, both residential and online.

While debates continue about what should be taught in museum studies programs, one thing remains certain: students will always need access to new and different approaches to museum studies, especially when that information is provided by highly respected museum professionals, with decades of experience in both the academic and day-to-day aspects of museum practice.

Kiersten Latham and John Simmons are uniquely qualified to write a museum studies textbook that offers a broad, holistic introduction to the field in an international context, interweaving museological theory and museum practice to show how each informs the other, to help museums change and grow to better serve their audiences. The concepts and ideas presented in this book have been selected and developed by the authors based on their experiences working in museums, and honed by their years of teaching museum studies to graduate students. Museum studies is presented from an information and library science perspective, using a systems approach to analyze museums as dynamic organizations. The result is an understanding of museums as evolving institutions embedded in a larger cultural complex that includes libraries, archives, and other information entities, emphasizing the importance of the object-based learning that takes place in museums.

Museums today fill many roles in societies around the world—as educational institutions, as research institutions, as economic engines for communities, as preservers of the world's great heritages, and as trusted conveners. If museums are to continue to help us understand the past and navigate our future—as individuals, as societies, and as a global community—then future museum professionals must understand the historical development of museums, the work of museums in a global context, the broad skill set required for a successful museum career, and the interaction of museums and museum professionals across the spectrum of academic disciplines. *Foundations of Museum Studies: Evolving Systems of Knowledge* provides an important introduction to museum studies and a solid foundation on which students can build their careers in the museum field.

Ford W. Bell, DVM
President
American Alliance of Museums
Washington, DC

Preface

Why This Book?

This book has evolved—like museums—for several reasons. First, we saw the need for a concise introduction to museums and museum studies. It has been many years since the *Manual for Museums* by Ralph H. Lewis (1976) and *Introduction to Museum Work* by G. Ellis Burcaw (first edition 1975, third edition 1997) were written. Although there have been other good books since those volumes appeared—most notably *Museums in Motion* by Mary Alexander and Edward P. Alexander (first edition 1979, second edition 2007)—none have filled the role of providing an integrated practice-and-theory-based, holistic introduction to museums and their study. A second impetus for writing this book was that one of us (KFL) developed an entirely new specialization in museum studies within the master of library and information science (MLIS) program at Kent State University in 2010–2011. This book is modeled on the introductory course Foundations of Museum Studies, which is the prerequisite for all other museum studies courses in the program. The third reason is that because library and information science (LIS) schools are beginning to incorporate the study of museums into their curricula, there is an increasing need to understand museums from this perspective (and vice versa). Finally, as graduates of museum studies programs ourselves, we wanted to write the sort of book that we wish had been available when we were graduate students.

What Is the Purpose of This Book?

This volume is meant to be the central text for an introductory graduate course on museum studies. It is our intention that it will give readers a broad overview of museums, from their early history to the present (and with speculation on their future); explain how museums function; and provide a good understanding of the theoretical bases of museum studies. It is meant to be an introduction that lends itself well to supplementary readings assigned by the instructor to delve more deeply into the many complex crevices of museum studies.

How Is This Book Different?

Although it was written from within an LIS school, the perspective and framework found in this book are broad enough that all institutions of learning that teach introductory museum studies can use it. One of the unique things about the book is that we take a systems perspective on museums and consider them document-centered institutions. In doing this, we have brought both museums and museum studies together and have examined museum practice through the interdisciplinary lenses of theory. We see museums as part of the spectrum of educational, informational, and recreational institutions that includes libraries, archives, special collections, and others and feel that they deserve inclusion as such. In addition, although our perspective on museums is global (between us we have worked with museums in countries around the globe), we know museums in the United States best; therefore many of our examples are from U.S. institutions. What this book is not is a detailed manual on how to run a museum—information on the step-by-step details of museum practice is available elsewhere.

How to Use This Book

This book is arranged in the order of subject matter that we follow in the Foundations of Museum Studies course at Kent State University, which is organized around the simple questions how, what, who, where, and why. The order and content has evolved over several years of teaching and practice into what we believe is the best approach for an introduction to the subject. We have supplemented the text with photographs and figures to provide further understanding. In addition, sprinkled throughout the text are a series of "Reality Checks" that provide our personal perspectives on the intersection of theory and practice in museums.

Although we have kept the number of references minimal, we encourage instructors and students to supplement the text with other readings, particularly those that focus more specifically on current and trending issues, because museum studies is a rapidly evolving field. The growth of the museum studies literature since the 1970s has been tremendous, and anyone interested in a career in museum work will profit from reading widely and copiously.

What Is in This Book?

Our book begins with a critical examination of the many definitions of museums and our proposal of a definition that we believe works best, followed by a review of the history of museums and how they have evolved and changed over the centuries. In Section Two (How) we examine museums as systems and how the museum system is situated within other, larger systems. Although many museum studies textbooks have treated museums as if they were independent, stand-alone institutions, we want readers to see museums as integral parts of the societies in which they function. The next chapter in this section presents an overview of the essential functions of museums: preservation of collections, research, and communication. The two chapters in Section Three (What) address critical issues found in the many kinds of museums that exist today, the commonalities they share, the differences that distinguish them, and what we call the *meaningful physical resource*—the objects in museums. Most museum studies texts treat objects as merely things that make up the collections, focusing on the prescriptive aspects of how objects are managed in collections. However, we consider both the physicality and the meaning of objects, particularly how these meanings evolve when objects become musealized. This section includes the heart of our book, an examination of the critical shift in museology from a primary focus on museum visitors to a primary focus on the relationship between people and objects, and in that context, how objects are used and perceived, what they signify, and how they act as documents. Section Four (Who) looks at the human aspects of museums, both the museum workers (in Chapter 7) and the museum users (Chapter 8). Section Five (Where) reviews the evolving concept of museums as they have sprouted up all over the world. The last portion of the book, Section Six (Why), gives readers a glimpse of what lies ahead for them in their careers and a place to think intentionally about their own role in shaping the future of museums.

Who Are We?

Kiersten F. Latham earned a BA in anthropology, an MA in historical administration and museum studies, and a PhD in library and information management. During her professional career, she has held a variety of museum positions that have brought her in close contact with a myriad of museum types and sizes, including director of a local historical society, curator of collections and research at a city museum, curator of collections at a space history museum, program coordinator at a science center, costumed interpreter at a living history museum, and acting director of the University of Kansas Museum Studies Program. Latham has also served as an adjunct faculty member for Bethany College, University of Kansas, Northern States Conservation Center, Michigan State University, and Bowling Green State University. In 2010 she accepted a position at Kent State University as assistant professor in the School of Library and Information Science (SLIS), where she designed, developed, and implemented a museum studies specialization situated within an information perspective. Latham conducts research and has published extensively in the areas of museology, document studies, lived experience, materiality, and phenomenological research methods. Her publications include *The Invisibility of Collections Care Work* (2007), *Archives and Experience: Musings on Meaning* (2007), *The Poetry of the Museum: A Holistic Model of Numinous Museum Experiences* (2007), *Museum Object as Document: Using Buckland's Information Concepts to Understand Museum Experiences* (2012), *The Thickness of the Things: Exploring the Museum Curriculum through Phenomenological Touch* (2011, with E. Wood), and *The Objects of Experience: Transforming Visitor-Object Encounters in Museums* (2013, with E. Wood), among others.

John E. Simmons has a BS in systematics and ecology and an MA in historical administration and museum studies. He began his career as a zookeeper, then worked as collections manager at the California Academy of Sciences and the Biodiversity Research Center and Natural History Museum of the University of Kansas, where he also served as director of the Museum Studies Program. Currently he teaches museum studies as an adjunct faculty member at the Universidad Nacional de Colombia, Juniata College, Kent State University, and the Northern States Conservation Center; serves as adjunct curator of collections at the Earth and Mineral Sciences Museum & Art Gallery at Penn State University; and runs Museologica, an international museum consulting company. Simmons received the Superior Voluntary Service Award from AAM (2001), the Chancellor's Award for Outstanding Mentoring of Graduate Students from the University of Kansas (2005), and the Carolyn L. Rose Award for Outstanding Commitment to Natural History Collections Care and Management from the Society for the Preservation of Natural History Collections (2011). Among his publications are *Herpetological Collecting and Collections Management* (2002), *Cuidado, Manejo y Conservación de las Colecciones Biológicas* (2005, with Yaneth Muñoz-Saba), *Things Great and Small: Collections Management Policies* (2006), *History of Museums* (2010), *Observation and Distillation— Perception, Depiction, and the Perception of Nature* (2012, with Julianne Snider), and *Application of Preventive Conservation to Solve the Coming Crisis in Collections Management* (2013).

References

Alexander, Edward P., and Mary Alexander. 2008. *Museums in Motion: An Introduction to the History and Functions of Museums*. 2nd ed. Lanham, MD: Altamira Press.

Burcaw, G. Ellis. 1997. *Introduction to Museum Work*. 3rd ed. Walnut Creek, CA: Altamira Press.

Latham, Kiersten F. 2007a. "The Invisibility of Collections Care Work." *Collections* 3, no. 1: 103–112.

Latham, Kiersten F. 2007b. "Archives and Experience: Musings on Meaning." *Collections* 3, no. 2: 125–133.

Latham, Kiersten F. 2007c. "The Poetry of the Museum: A Holistic Model of Numinous Museum Experiences." *Museum Management and Curatorship* 22, no. 3: 247–263.

Latham, Kiersten F. 2012. "Museum Object as Document: Using Buckland's Information Concepts to Understand Museum Experiences." *Journal of Documentation* 68, no. 2: 45–71.

Latham, Kiersten F., and Elizabeth Wood. 2011. "The Thickness of the Things: Exploring the Museum Curriculum through Phenomenological Touch." *Journal of Curriculum Theorizing* 27, no. 2: 51–65.

Lewis, Ralph H. 1975. *Manual for Museums*. Washington, DC: National Park Service, U.S. Department of the Interior.

Rubin, Richard. 2010. *Foundations of Library and Information Science*. New York: Neal-Schuman Publishers.

Simmons, John E. 2002. *Herpetological Collecting and Collections Management*. Rev. ed. Herpetological Circular no. 31. n.p.: Society for the Study of Amphibians and Reptiles.

Simmons, John E. 2006. *Things Great and Small: Collections Management Policies*. Washington, DC: American Association of Museums.

Simmons, John E. 2010. "History of Museums." In *Encyclopedia of Library and Information Sciences*, 3rd ed., edited by Marcia J. Bates and Mary Niles Maack, 2096–2106. London: Taylor and Francis.

Simmons, John E. 2013. "Application of Preventive Conservation to Solve the Coming Crisis in Collections Management." *Collection Forum* 27, nos. 1–2: 89–101.

Simmons, John E., and Yaneth Muñoz-Saba. 2005. *Cuidado, Manejo y Conservación de las Colecciones Biológicas*. Bogota: Instituto de Ciencias Naturales, Facultad de Ciencias, Universidad Nacional de Colombia, Conservación Internacional, Ministerio de Ambiente, Vivienda y Desarrollo Territorial, Fondo para la Acción Ambiental.

Simmons, John E., and Julianne Snider. 2012. "Observation and Distillation— Perception, Depiction, and the Perception of Nature." *Bibliotheca Herpetologica*, 9, nos. 1–2: 115–134.

Wood, Elizabeth, and Kiersten F. Latham. 2013. *The Objects of Experience: Transforming Visitor-Object Encounters in Museums*. Walnut Creek, CA: Left Coast Press.

Acknowledgments

A great deal of work goes into the making of a textbook. Many people have been involved along the way, and to all of them, we are grateful.

First, we thank our publisher, ABC-CLIO, for recognizing the need for this textbook and giving us the freedom to develop this book amid our often busy and conflicting schedules.

We greatly appreciate Cori Iannaggi, Randy Brown, Emily Wicks, Elee Wood, Teresa Goforth, and Brad Taylor, Blanche Woolls, and an anonymous reviewer for their critical comments and helpful suggestions on the manuscript. Thanks also to John Gouin (Graphikitchen) for his creative graphic interpretations, and to Julianne Snider for her assistance in selecting and formatting the photographs.

K. F. Latham: I would like to thank my colleagues and friends at Kent State School of Library and Information Science for patiently listening to me talk about this book for two years and to my students—from Kent State and before—who helped form the structure and form of the book through their feedback and questions along the way. Thanks are also due to John Agada, Greg Byerly, and Carolyn Brodie for having the vision to include museum studies in the field of library and information science and having the faith in me to make a difference. Special gratitude goes out to many colleagues who, during more than twenty years of working in various museums, taught me how to understand how museums work and what they are all about. This book would not have been possible without the existence of my wonderful co-author, John Simmons, who has been my teacher, mentor, and colleague for almost as long as I've been in the museum field. Most of all, I want to thank my dear husband, Mark, and sweet child, Callan, for listening to Mama go on endlessly about museum studies even though they might rather have talked about archaeology, basketball, *Doctor Who*, or *Sherlock*.

J. E. Simmons: I thank Julianne Snider for her suggestions, assistance, and patience during the writing of this book; I could not have done my part without her steadfast help and support. I owe a great debt of gratitude to Kiersten F. Latham for recruiting me to teach museum studies at Kent State, for introducing me to the ideas of Ivo Maroević, and most of all for inviting me to participate in the writing of this book. Teaching is something I never intended to take on, but I am very grateful for the opportunities I have had to convey my fascination with museums to students. Nearly forty years of working in museums and in the classroom (both analog and virtual) has proved over and over again that one always learns more from teaching than from being a student.

Section One
Introduction

1

Defining Museums
(and Museum Studies)

What Is a Museum?

Before exploring the ins and outs of museum studies, it is necessary to establish some basic definitions. Most people probably have some idea of what a museum is, but upon closer consideration, it is not a simple, clear-cut issue. The shades of grey discussed here are the defining elements of museums—complexity and diversity are among the characteristics that make museums unique institutions in society. This chapter begins with an exploration of the etymology of the word *museum* and then examines some current definitions of the institution, before arriving at a working definition that is used throughout this book. The parameters of museum studies as a field are considered in the second half of the chapter.

Etymology of the Word *Museum*

The word *museum* is derived from the Greek word *mouseion*, meaning the place where the muses dwell. The muses were sister-goddesses responsible for entrancing and inspiring literature, science, and the arts, and were believed to be the sources of knowledge for poets, musicians, historians, dancers, astronomers, and others. Although the Temple of the Muses, the *Mouseion*—an institution founded by Ptolemy Soter in the third century BC in Alexandria—was more like a university than a museum by today's standards, it represents the first formal association of objects and learning. Although the *Mouseion* wasn't open to the public in the modern sense, it was open to learned professors and their students.

The word *museum* appeared in the fifteenth century in reference to the collections of the Medici family in Florence, Italy, who are credited by some as the creators of the first museum (Hooper-Greenhill 1992). The first published use of the word *museum* in English occurred in 1615 in a travel book by George Sandys (1578–1644), referring to the ruins of the Temple of the Muses in Alexandria: "that famous Musaeum founded by Philadelphus" and "that renowned Library" (the Library of Alexandria). From the 1600s onward the word museum was used to refer to institutions that collected and exhibited objects.

Defining Museum

Note that while there are many definitions of the word *museum*, there is no general agreement (by those who work in, with, and on museums) about what makes a museum a museum. Throughout history people have questioned the purpose of museums, and they still do so today. The reason for this is really quite simple; museums are dynamic institutions that respond to societal trends, beliefs, and cultural paradigms. It is therefore important to note that a single definition is not set in stone, nor is there agreement today on the ultimate description defining that institution, *museum*. Therefore, it is important to consider a variety of definitions before settling on one. To arrive at a working definition for this book, two sets of descriptions are evaluated: (1) the definitions of museums from professional organizations and (2) models of museums.

Definitions from Professional Organizations

When defining what a museum is, many people look to the major professional organizations for guidance. A professional association is an organization formed to unite and inform people who work in the same occupation, help establish and maintain standards, act as a communicative body, and represent shared beliefs about the profession in discussions with other bodies. The definitions offered by several core museum organizations from around the world are examined below.

This is the International Council of Museums' current definition of museum, according to the ICOM Statutes (adopted at the 21st General Conference in 2007):

> A museum is a non-profit, permanent institution in the service of society and its development, open to the public, which acquires, conserves, researches, communicates and exhibits the tangible and intangible heritage of humanity and its environment for the purposes of education, study, and enjoyment. (ICOM n.d.)

The American Alliance of Museums (AAM; formerly the American Association of Museums) does not have an official definition of *museum*, but considers organizations such as archaeological parks (Figure 1.1), zoological parks (Figure 1.2), and botanical gardens (Figure 1.3) to be museums. The AAM accreditation committee does have a definition of museum that it has used since the 1970s, which states that a museum is

> an organized and permanent nonprofit institution, essentially educational or esthetic in a purpose, with professional staff, that owns or uses tangible objects, cares for them and exhibits them to the public on some regular schedule. (quoted in Alexander and Alexander 2008)

Further insight into this organization's notion of *museum* can be found in the AAM list of accreditation criteria (American Alliance of Museums 2013) which, among other things, states that a museum must

Figure 1.1 An archaeological site as a museum: Prasat Hin Phimai Historic Park (Phimai, Thailand). Photograph by the authors.

- be a legally organized nonprofit institution or part of a nonprofit organization or government entity;

- be essentially educational in nature;

- have a formally stated and approved mission;

- use and interpret objects and/or be a site for the public presentation of regularly scheduled programs and exhibits;

Figure 1.2   Is a zoo a museum? Giraffes enjoying a sunny day at the Taronga Park Zoo in Sydney, Australia. Photograph by the authors.

Figure 1.3   Is a botanical garden a museum? The Hortus Botanicus in Leiden (The Netherlands) is one of the oldest botanical gardens in the world. Photograph by the authors.

- have a formal and appropriate program of documentation, care, and use of collections and/or objects;
- carry out the above functions primarily at a physical facility/site;
- have been open to the public for at least two years;
- be open to the public at least 1,000 hours a year;
- have accessioned 80 percent of its permanent collection;
- have at least one paid professional staff member with museum knowledge and experience;
- have a full-time director to whom authority is delegated for day-to-day operations; and
- have financial resources sufficient to operate effectively.

The Canadian Museums Association (2013) offers another definition:

Museums are institutions created in the public interest. They engage their visitors, foster deeper understanding and promote the enjoyment and sharing of authentic cultural and natural heritage. Museums acquire, preserve, research, interpret and exhibit the tangible and intangible evidence of society and nature. As educational institutions, museums provide a physical forum for critical inquiry and investigation.

Finally, the United Kingdom's Museums Association (2013) states:

Museums enable people to explore collections for inspiration, learning and enjoyment. They are institutions that collect, safeguard and make accessible artefacts and specimens, which they hold in trust for society.

While it does not come from a professional organization, in the United States a legal definition of *museum* can be found in the legislation authorizing the establishment of the federal Institute of Museum Services (now the Institute of Museum and Library Services, or IMLS):

A public or private nonprofit agency or institution organized on a permanent basis for essentially educational or aesthetic purposes, which, utilizing a professional staff, owns or utilizes tangible objects, cares for them, and exhibits them to the public on a regular basis. (Museum Services Act 1976)

In all of these definitions, there are patterns and similarities, but also a few differences. The "public" is present in all whether they are to be exhibited to, educated, or entertained—what the museum does is for the public benefit or in the public interest. Another theme is the notion of material evidence, which is to be cared for, interpreted, and preserved. The last point that comes out in most of the professional definitions is that these activities are done in a regular and consistent manner by trained staff.

Museum Models

The definitions above are helpful, but they are very straightforward and lack nuance and detail. Museums are highly complicated institutions, so more detail is needed to arrive at an adequate definition for use in this book. To simplify a complicated issue, two broad categories that have been used to sort out museums from similar institutions—function and type—are considered here. Below are some of the common functions and types of museums:

Function: to collect, to conserve, to educate, to interpret, to exhibit, to research, to serve

Type: art, art center, anthropology, aquarium, arboretum, botanical garden, children's, herbarium, history, historic house, natural history, science center, science and technology, planetarium, gallery, zoo

It is human nature to divide and categorize, so each of these types of museums has developed its own character and culture. Although there is by no means a single way to describe an art museum, for example, there are certain things art museums have in common that set them apart from other museums. The collection of an art museum is quite different from that of a zoo or a history museum. Art carries with it its own interesting issues, including questions of what a particular work means, its relationship with the artist, and the notion of beauty. The same goes for other museums. For instance, natural history museums collect the natural evidence of the world, and with that comes classification, biological research, and vastly different storage issues.

At the same time, all museums have similar functions in common—such as collecting, cataloging, caring for collections, and interpreting them for the public—so although there are differences, there are also characteristics shared among even the most diverse types of institutions.

A thought-provoking article by Adam Gopnik presents an interesting and different way to model museums that might give us insight into their dynamic nature. In *The Mindful Museum* (2007) he describes five kinds of museums and considers them in a historical progression:

Museum as Mausoleum—a place where you go to see old things, to find yourself as an aesthete or scholar; above all a place connected to the past; a silent experience for the individual.

Museum as Machine—not mechanical, but productive; where you go to be transformed, to learn (about the present); you emerge informed, educated, changed; a place of quiet, significant instruction.

Museum as Metaphor—extravagant, flamboyant, romantic; a museum that no longer pursues an audience but provides us with a central arena of sociability.

Museum as Mall—exclusively devoted to pleasure; overcrowded, overmerchandised; the collection becomes a commodity.

Museum as Mindful—aware of itself; obviously and primarily about the objects it contains; objects are intrinsic to the experience; encourages conversation but does not force information.

Gopnik's point is that museums should strive to be mindful. Whether you agree with that assertion or not, it should be clear by now that museums are complex and that there really is no single kind of museum, or one single model that describes them all. In today's world, the museum must be adaptable and will probably serve multiple roles for varied audiences. Understanding the museum's functions must happen at one level; understanding the types of collections it holds will happen at another level; and whether it serves as mausoleum, machine, metaphor, mall, or mindful museum will depend on the time, the exhibit topics, the staff, the audience, and the programs. From one perspective or another, each of these kinds of museums may describe the same museum.

The Legal Organization of Museums

Before moving on to a working definition for this book, the position of the museum as a legal entity must be considered. In the United States, museums can be either public or private institutions. This distinction is important because it determines who owns the collections and who is legally liable for their care. Private museums are created by individuals and managed by a board and museum officers, but public museums are established and managed by federal, state, or local governments.

Most private museums have nonprofit status; are organized as tax-exempt organizations; are controlled by their members; and are organized as trusts, associations, or corporations. *Nonprofit* means that an organization is exempt from paying most taxes; it is operated for specific, stated purposes; and the money the organization earns is invested in the organization itself. By contrast, the money earned by a private, for-profit museum is paid to the museum's owners or shareholders. The main difference between nonprofit and for-profit museums is that the collections of nonprofit museums are held in the public trust, whereas the collections of for-profit museums are legally corporate assets that may be sold (and the proceeds may be paid to the owners or shareholders of the museum).

It is important to understand the differences between trusts, associations, and corporations when learning about museums. *Trusts* are arrangements in which the management of the trust property is the obligation of the trustees, for the benefit of the beneficiaries of the trust. In a museum, this means that the trustees (the board) have a legal obligation (and the power) to properly manage the museum (the trust property). *Associations* are unincorporated organizations that are formed by a group of members who agree to support a common purpose. Generally speaking, associations cannot receive or hold property. *Corporations* are legal entities that are created by and operated under the laws of a particular state and may acquire property in a way similar to how an individual can own property. The board of directors of a corporation does not have the same legal responsibilities as do the trustees of a trust—the board of a corporation has a duty to be loyal to the corporation, while the board of a trust has a duty to be loyal to the intention of the trust (Phelan 2014). In practice, this means that the board of a museum that is an organized trust does not have as much flexibility in how it runs the museum as does a museum that is organized as a nonprofit corporation, because the terms of the trust limit what the board can do. Most museums in the United States are organized as nonprofit corporations that hold their collections in the public trust.

A Working Definition

Alexander and Alexander (2008) point out that the fulcrum for the multiplicity of definitions seems to be between the museum as a repository for objects and the museum as a place for learning. Indeed, the contemporary

Figure 1.4   Keene's model of the museum system. Adapted from Keene (2002).

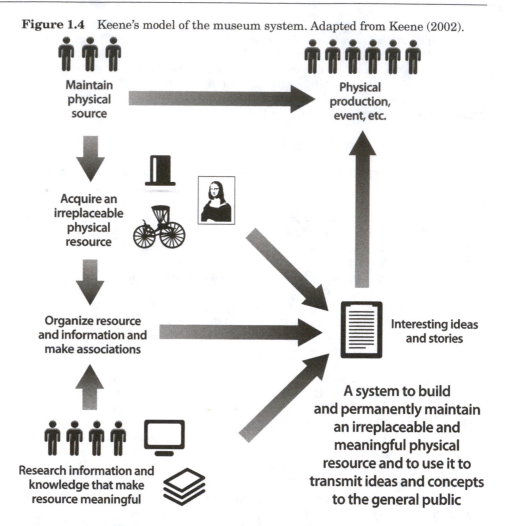

museum must manage a balancing act between these two important roles, as can be seen in the elements present in all the definitions above. In an attempt to make these two facets work together more clearly, Keene defines a museum as "a system to build and permanently maintain an irreplaceable and meaningful physical resource and to use it to transmit ideas and concepts to the public" (2002, 90). In Keene's view, a museum is not simply a place with objects that are accessible to everyone, because the accessible things act in a system of inputs and outputs, which involves particular processes and takes into account outside pressures from the world (see Figure 1.4).

As Keene points out, a museum is not an island, but exists within a complex web of societal expectations, past traditions, and interwoven levels of meaning. Because Keene's definition takes into account all of these things—systems, external influences, inputs (objects and information), outputs (exhibits, programs), people—it is used throughout this book to discuss museums.

Museum: a system to build and permanently maintain an irreplaceable and meaningful physical resource and use it to transmit ideas and concepts to the public.

Keep in mind that this is not the perfect definition of a museum; there are debatable portions, such as the notion of permanence and the seemingly unidirectional nature of transmission, which are tackled in other sections of this book. Two components of this definition are reviewed next: the public and the meaningful physical resource. Chapter 3 delves further into the system that builds and maintains these components.

The Public

It seems axiomatic that museums exist to serve the public. But if museums do exist to serve the public, how do they do it, and who is *the public*? What makes some museums public museums and others private—and do both actually serve *the public*? These are not idle questions, as sometimes the museum board doesn't do its duty and neglects to properly manage the museum as a public trust; when this happens, the board can be held legally responsible for its failure of duty. Knowing what *public* means in this definition is crucial at all levels, including understanding the concept of public trust and the social responsibilities of museums in society.

What Is the Public Trust?

Since the advent of democracy, the idea that certain activities are carried out for the benefit of the public has been a broadly used (though complicated) concept. While the idea of a public trust is not unique to the United States, it plays a more significant role in public institutions here than in most other countries. In the United States the concept of public trust is at the center of defining museums. From the museum perspective, public trust can be seen in two ways: legally (as an aspect of common law) and conceptually (as an ethical concern).

The nonprofit museum has a fiduciary relationship with the public, meaning that the museum holds property (the collections) that is administered for the benefit of others (the public) (Malaro and DeAngelis 2012). This relationship means that no one individual can use the property for personal gain, and that the assets can only benefit the group that is the beneficiary of the trust. Museum officials serve as the *trustees*, and the public are the *beneficiaries*. Malaro and DeAngelis (2012) make the point, based on legal standards, that museums have a duty of care, a duty of loyalty, and a duty of obedience to their beneficiaries. Because museums exist to protect, preserve, and increase the trust's assets, museums in the United States are said to operate *in the public trust*. This relationship is tightly wrapped up with the second meaning of public trust as an ethical concern.

Public trust museums in the United States are grounded in the notion of public service: museums hold their collections as public trusts, as a benefit to those they were established to serve (e.g., as outlined in the AAM Code of Ethics). But upholding public trust responsibilities entails more than simply following the law. It means that museums must be loyal to their missions and must garner the respect and integrity necessary to warrant public confidence. This is where a code of ethics comes in. Professional ethics are guidelines for behavior that are based on experience and refined by being tested through experience. The purpose of a code of ethics is to raise the level of professional practice to a standard that is above the law. The idea of a code of ethics for museum professionals dates back to 1892, when George Brown Goode, the secretary of the Smithsonian Institution, proposed that museums should formulate standards of correct and ethical behavior and professional duty. The first formal code of ethics for museum professionals, *Code of Ethics for Museum Workers*, published by the American Association of Museums, was adopted in 1925. It was based on the practical wisdom and collective experience of people working in museums. The AAM code was revised in 1987 and again in 1993–1994. Another significant code of ethics for museums is the ICOM code, first promulgated in 1986 and revised in 2004, which is widely followed by non-U.S. museums.

Social Responsibility

A perennial issue that confronts museums, particularly public museums, is the role that they should play in society. Should museums be passive holders of knowledge that store, preserve, and display objects and just give basic information to the public? Or should museums take an active role in bringing issues, sometimes controversial, to the fore? Should museums be catalysts for asking questions, inspiring and producing new knowledge, and stimulating dialogue?

Community and social responsibility have become increasingly important to the usefulness and value of today's museum institutions. *Community responsibility* refers to more local involvement in one's own constituency. Many museums have become more involved in their communities and in return have asked for more involvement from them. Support from locals, as both visitors and volunteers, may be the difference between staying open and closing the doors of a museum. Depending on the kind of museum, funding sources may be entirely local, and forging a good relationship with one's neighbors may help increase the long-term value of the site.

Social responsibility refers to a larger purpose, a national or perhaps cultural duty to the museum's overall audience, present and future. Some museums have begun to view their role in society as being an active question-asking entity, a place where assumptions are questioned and issues are raised. Some museums go so far as to position themselves to intentionally address controversial issues. In the past, many museums in the United States took a somewhat passive role when it came to controversy. They would either stay away from hot issues or only present "the facts," the safer components of a story. Today some museums continue this pattern, but others have chosen to stimulate conversation by purposefully designing contentious exhibitions.

The Meaningful Physical Resource

Museums are stewards of the world's natural and cultural common resources and are therefore compelled to advance understanding and foster appreciation of that diverse world and how to preserve it. Many people tend to associate museums with a particular subject-matter, content, or discipline, but as can be seen from the above exploration with respect to defining the institution, the subject-matter is not the whole picture. Collecting objects of a certain period, place, type, or association is important and relates to the all-important mission. However, the meaningful physical resource is more than subject-matter: institutions must *have or use* objects, provide public access to those objects in some way, and be open to present them on a regular basis in order to *be* museums. The objects themselves are what make a museum. Other institutions do not put physical, three-dimensional collections at the center of their functioning the way museums do. This positioning makes the museum a unique institution in society. Even so, this aspect of the museum definition continues to be contested, especially in the digital age. The following discussion introduces several issues surrounding the collection that have been the topic of much debate in museums: whether the museum needs to own a physical collection of objects, what those objects mean in the museum context, and the role of the virtual in a physical world.

Collection Required?

The presence or absence of collections as a defining characteristic of a museum has been debated in the museum community for a number of years. Many institutions that do not own collections but exhibit them are considered museums because of the interpretive, educational, and public nature of their programs; these institutions, after all, *use* objects to do this work. This leads to the question: Must an institution own a collection in order to be a museum? Or does *using* objects (the individual contents of a collection) also count? For example, what about a science center? Such institutions are usually centered around "hands-on" activities designed to instruct visitors about some aspect of the physical universe, but often the only objects they hold are the reproductions, models, and interactives built for the specific purpose of teaching various concepts. Nevertheless, these exhibits are filled with physical, three-dimensional representations used to demonstrate such concepts. In other words, these institutions *use objects*, a meaningful physical resource, to transmit ideas and concepts to the public. Even though the objects in these institutions are not preserved and are not specifically representative of some time, culture, or species, they are nevertheless integral to the concept of the museum. In the end, science centers *use objects to convey ideas to their audiences*. Keene's definition, however, says that these physical resources must be irreplaceable. Is this necessary, or is the use of replaceable objects just as valid?

Some institutions have objects that many would not immediately perceive as parts of collections or might even find difficult to call *objects*. For example, zoos hold collections of animals. Are zoos museums? Zoos collect, systematically care for their collections (live ones though they be), educate the public about them, and are regularly open to the public.

Yet another species of potential museum are those institutions that hold collections but do not provide public access to them. As an example, the Museum of Vertebrate Paleontology at the University of California in Berkeley contains thousands of fossil specimens but is not considered a museum (according to most definitions) because it has no exhibits open to the public. The Web site for the museum includes virtual exhibits, but there are no physical exhibits. Some people would argue that having a Web site makes the collection publicly accessible, and that virtual exhibitions are the equivalent of three-dimensional exhibits in the transmission of ideas and concepts to the public, per Keene's definition.

Access vs. Meaning

In today's world, many key issues for libraries, archives, and museums boil down to access versus meaning. The digital revolution has made possible greater access to more things than ever before in human history. For example, archival institutions can digitize their materials and make them available on a Web site for anyone in the world to access. If you are doing your family's genealogy from Cape Town, South Africa, you may not have to fly 8,800 miles to Virginia to find out about your great-great grandfather who emigrated to America in 1895. If the appropriate materials have been digitized and made accessible by an archival institution in Virginia, you can access them from your dining room table in Cape Town. There is a sense of freedom with this incredible access, but there is evidence that accessing the material online is different than actually experiencing the material—physical access provides a different kind of information to users. For example, Duff and Cherry (2000) found that people distinguished between getting information from an actual document versus seeing a digital image of the document. They reported that 41.3 percent of the participants who used original paper, microfiche, and digital formats liked the paper format most—some saying that the experience was qualitatively different if they were in the same room with the object and could hold it in their hands. These physical object experiences are generally more meaningful to people and can leave deep impressions on their memories, perceptions, and emotions. Recent work by Latham (2009, 2013) found that deeply felt experiences with museum objects were more meaningful to people when they were in the presence of the physical things rather than through some other representation of them. In these examples, people distinguished between quick, convenient access to information and meaningful, more deeply connective experiences; it is almost as if the two are on opposite ends of a spectrum.

An example that reveals the complex nature of access and meaning is the Google Art Project, through which anyone from anywhere in the world can access paintings from around the globe and zoom in to see artworks closer even than a visitor could while physically standing in front of them. Although the viewer is not in the same physical space as the object, there is a certain level of intimate access through the Google Art Project that one cannot achieve when in the actual presence of the artworks. The Google Art Project allows a user to zoom very close to a painting, close enough that the brushstrokes can be seen (an important feature mentioned by those in the Latham study who were discussing meaningful physical encounters). While it has yet to be demonstrated whether or not this creates similar meaning for users, it does provide a level of access that is deeper than has been seen previously in other digitally accessed material.

The Virtual Museum

Much debate and discussion surrounds the concept of the virtual museum. This is not a simple issue, as what is considered *virtual* in the museum context actually falls on a continuum from a collection of digitized objects available online to an immersion experience utilizing high-tech equipment to make people feel as if they were *in* a museum. Several years ago, many museums jumped on the Second Life bandwagon, taking advantage of what they thought would be new paths to reach untapped audiences. Many of these ventures did not amount to much, and few of these virtual museums have endured. Still, some worry that the virtual version will someday replace the physical version of the museum, although this concern seems to be subsiding as it becomes clear that humans continue to need physical and social interactions in the presence of actual objects. Others contend that the physical museum—the building, objects, people, and exhibits—will always be more important to society than a virtual representation. It is difficult to predict what will happen, because a younger generation is growing up more accustomed to virtual and digital access. How will this affect the future of the physical museum as technology allows greater (and different kinds of) access to museums and their collections?

It is less expensive and perhaps easier (or at least quicker) to build virtual exhibitions than to build physical ones. Digital storage of objects is far less expensive than physical storage, which requires infrastructure, labor, and maintenance. It is indeed tantalizing to consider such efficiency. But physical collections provide something that cannot be found in digital form, as discussed above. Several studies cite the importance of seeing the real thing (e.g., Moore 1997; Reach 2004; Latham 2014) and being in the presence of a complete exhibit, surrounded by artifacts, design, lights, colors, and sounds. Furthermore, research by Falk and Dierking (1992, 2000) and others has shown that learning in museums is mediated by the social group that the visitor is part of during the museum visit, but virtual visits almost always lack this dimension of the experience. The jury is still out on the question of physical versus virtual museums, but it is an important one for anyone entering the museum field to consider carefully and thoughtfully.

What Is Museum Studies?

Museum studies is a broad, multi- and interdisciplinary field that involves both theory and practice. It is a community that shares common values, allowing its various subdivisions to filter into each other, maintaining and feeding the connection through a common focus on underlying similarities. In library and information science (LIS), this is referred to as a discourse community. Just as defining the word museum is complicated, the terminology surrounding museum studies is equally complex. The traditional meaning of *museology* in English refers to the study of museums. In international use, however, museology is more often used to refer to "anything relating to museums" (Desvallées and Mairesse 2010), which includes museum studies. In English, *museography* is traditionally defined as the description of the contents of a museum, but in international use museography refers to the practical (applied) aspects of museology, or "the techniques which have been developed to fulfill museal operations" (Desvallées and Mairesse 2010). For purposes of this book, museum studies includes both museology (theory) and museography (practice).

> Museum studies = Museology (theory) + Museography (practice).

The next portion considers the character of museum studies, how museum professionals are trained, and the relationship between theory and practice in the field, then explores the notion of museum studies as a science and the unique terminology that belongs to this field.

The Character of the Field

It has already been shown just how complex and varied museums are as institutions. This complexity continues in the field that studies museums and trains its professionals. Museum studies traverses many disciplines and comprises both theory and practice. It is characterized by a history that continues to drive the training of its professionals as well as the inquiries it makes. The field is as dynamic and rich as the types and functions of

Figure 1.5   A conceptual model of museum studies. From Simmons (2006).

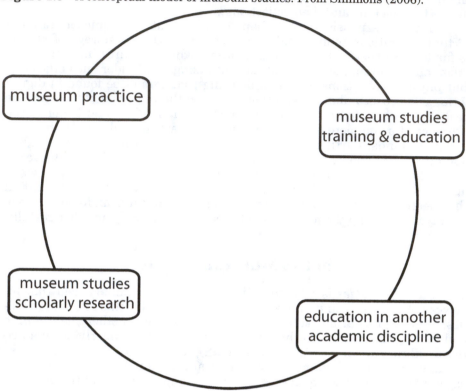

museums found within its purview. While it is difficult to make a sweeping statement about its character, there are a few core features of museum studies (and the institutions it examines) that characterize and therefore drive and sculpt the nature of inquiries undertaken. Museum studies can be characterized by six features:

- It is inherently interdisciplinary.
- It is a combination of theory and its application in practice.
- It acknowledges that much of the work undertaken in museums is hidden or taken for granted.
- The museum community that is studied is small and close-knit, yet subdivided into many traditional categories.
- Networking and the free and open sharing of information are characteristic of the museum community.
- Because so many collections are held in the public trust, the museum community strives for transparency and accountability.

A conceptual model of the field that integrates the many, often disparate, elements of museum studies (practice, training and education, scholarly research, and education in another discipline) is provided as Figure 1.5.

Although there is still some disagreement within the U.S. museum community about whether or not a degree in museum studies is the best training for the profession, the prevalence of museum studies programs in the United States and internationally indicates how highly the academic discipline of museum studies is now valued. Through a combination of coursework and hands-on experience, many museum studies programs have attempted to resolve the dilemma of whether museum work is best learned in an experiential or academic framework by combining the two in a model that emphasizes interdisciplinary approaches, research, theory, and practice.

Theory and Practice in Museum Studies

Why does museum studies need theory? Does museum studies need its own terminology? A theory provides a frame of reference for analyzing and synthesizing ideas and concepts, a means of comparing and contrasting, and a context for rigorous analysis. Theory is often seen as the opposite of practice, but in truth, practice should be the application of theory and theory should be looking to practice to know what questions to ask. The opposition between theory and practice "is as old as Western philosophy itself" (Macey 2000, 379). In modern practice, theory became established in the 1950s and 1960s as an alternative means of analysis to skepticism and empiricism. What would theory be applied to if there were no practice, and how would practice continue to grow, evolve, and progress without the conceptual investigations of theory to draw upon?

For many years museums have been immersed in the practical application of how to collect, preserve, study, and exhibit objects (Maroević 2000). According to Teather (1991), much museum research exists as primary research presented without a framework (or presented by borrowing other disciplines' frameworks) rather than being formed from the domains of museum studies thought and method. Even so, museum practitioners tend not to access theory, and if they do, they often are uncomfortable with jargon that may be difficult to make sense of in the context of their own working lives.

Since Teather (1991) pointed out the lack of a framework more than twenty years ago, a lot has happened in museum theory. Both the quantity of museum field-specific literature and the kind of research emerging show that the museum field is creating its own self-sustaining body of work. Furthermore, studies (e.g., Rounds 2001) show that the field does not show signs of dividing itself between those who produce museum theory (academics) and those who perform practical museum work (practitioners); rather, both sets of workers share and use each other's work.

Museum professionals seem to subscribe to a common understanding of what museum studies means, even if that meaning remains tacit. At the same time, the field is subdivided into groups based on content (types) and practice (jobs) that form their own character and knowledge webs. This is not to say that the groups do not communicate. It is important to note that, although the field may be divided into many specializations, these subdivisions are all connected, in practice and in theory.

At the heart of this divide is intentionality. Museum practitioners who use skills and techniques without a philosophy of work are not being intentional about their work. Where theory, or conceptual thinking, becomes important in museum work is in the intentional choices and awareness of those choices about how to do work that take it to a different level. This means that theory feeds practice and practice feeds theory—in a feedback loop.

Is Museum Studies a Science or an Art?

The distinction between science and art can be confusing, as each of these words means many things to many people. Broadly speaking, science refers to the application of systematic, organized, and objective principles; by contrast, art refers to nonsystematic, creative endeavors. Maroević (1998) extends this dichotomy to differentiate between cultural information, which he characterizes as synthetic, and scientific information, which he characterizes as analytic. In this broader sense, museum studies (which has a theoretical basis) is a science; by contrast, much of museum practice can be said to be an art.

One of the arguments for why museum studies is not a science is that it consists mostly of practical work and therefore does not have a unique body of theory. This argument extends to the question of whether or not museum studies can be called a discipline, a debate that has been raging almost since museum studies entered the academic scene in the early 1900s. In 1991 Teather called for a stop to this "tired" dispute (409), claiming that it is counterproductive and takes attention away from substantive discussions about the field of study. Teather's point is important, because museum studies includes *both* theory and practice, as pointed out above. Nevertheless, the debate continues despite the fact that it has been repeatedly demonstrated that museum studies is a scientific discipline grounded in its own transdisciplinary body of conceptual knowledge. (The evidence for this includes the growing number of publications and the number of scholars who study museums as museums, rather than the content of museums.)

Because science is systematic and organized inquiry about the world, museum studies is a science and a clearly defined field of study. With museality (see below) at the center of inquiry, museum studies has an extensive body of literature unique to its own topics and a group of scholars dedicated to asking museological questions who use theory from other fields (learning theory, design theory, information science, etc.) to their advantage and both feed on and learn from practice.

The "M" Words: Museality, Musealization, and Musealia

Specialized terminology is critical to a field for the discussion of unique concepts that arise in professional dialogue. Although museum studies has drawn much of its terminology from other fields (because of its highly interdisciplinary nature), several important concepts have grown out of the study of museums that have produced new vocabulary. In the 1970s the European museology community began to develop the new science of museum studies. Among the concepts that were articulated during this exploration are the terms *museal, musealia, musealization,* and *museality.* This terminology has become important in European and Latin American museum studies literature. *Museal* means "of museums." *Museality* is "the characteristic of something that in one reality documents another reality" (Stransky in Van Mensch 1992). Museal can be used as an adjective to qualify certain aspects of something or to describe the field of reference in which creation, development, and operation of the museum as an institution take place. *Musealia* refers to the objects that are the heritage of humanity, those things that are chosen to document some event, person, time, or idea (musealia includes artifacts, biological specimens, historic sites, and more). *Musealization* describes the processes by which an object becomes part of musealia. In referring to a "specific aspect of reality" (Stransky in Van Mensch 1990), the concept of museality has been used as a theoretical point of reference meant to frame thinking about objects of culture. The concept is useful in understanding the role of museum objects, the meaning of collecting, and human experience with things. Museal things, however, are not necessarily only found in museums; museal can refer to things outside of a museum that have been musealized, such as monuments, sites, buildings, and even cities. The use of this suite of terms (they are referred to as the "M words" in this book) has generally not taken hold in U.S. museum studies programs, and especially not in U.S. museum practice. But in actual application and use, these unique terms are very useful in the museum context.

Why Museum Studies in LIS?

In this book, museums are discussed as systems (Chapter 3), objects as documents (Chapter 6), exhibits as ecologies, and so forth. Much of this conceptual structure is drawn from the extensive world of LIS, which includes the study of libraries, archives, information science, user experience design, document studies, informatics, knowledge management, and more. With further exploration, one can see that museums naturally fall within the purview of LIS studies, an approach many European LIS schools have been taking for years. Recently Marcia Bates, a well-known LIS scholar, offered a framework for understanding information professions in light of societal, technological, and cognitive changes that have occurred in the past few years (Bates 2012). Building on her previous work (e.g., Bates 1999), she noted that some fields cut across the traditional spectrum of content disciplines (e.g., the arts, humanities, social and behavioral sciences, natural science, and math):

> There are some fields, however, that cut all the way across this spectrum; they deal with every traditional subject matter, but do so from a particular perspective. These fields organize themselves around some particular social purpose or interest, which then becomes the lens through which the subject fields, such as literature, geology, etc., are regarded. There are both theoretical and research questions to study, looking through that lens, and practical, professional matters to address. I call these fields "meta-disciplines." (Bates 2012, 2)

These meta-disciplines include, for example, information disciplines, communication, journalism, and education. The information disciplines focus on the collection, organization, retrieval, use, representation, and presentation of information in diverse contexts and situations, potentially cutting across all traditional disciplines. LIS—and museum studies within it—are meta-disciplines. Bates says that all information disciplines are becoming more applicable to a broader range of information solutions as people begin to understand them in this light. In fact, the 2010 edition of the *Encyclopedia of Library and Information Sciences* includes an entry for museum studies.

LAM: The Convergence of Libraries, Archives, and Museums

While Bates and others have been discussing the meta-disciplines, there has been a movement dubbed the "convergence of the LAMs," an acronym for libraries, archives, and museums. Traditionally, libraries, archives, and museums have divided their content into "piecemeal offerings" based on the nature and focus of their collections (Zorich, Waibel, and Erway 2008, 8). In recent years, however, the desire to bring these different, yet interrelated, services together has gained prominence. At its core, the goal of convergence is to create a system that will allow access to information across all collections in either a unified digital system or, in some cases, a single physical location. This spirit of collaboration is driven by the desire to create a fuller, more comprehensive experience for users of these institutions.

According to Given and McTavish (2010), the current trend toward convergence is more accurately described as reconvergence. In the late 1800s and early 1900s, libraries, archives, and museums often shared space, resources, and personnel. Over time, changes in funding, education, and public perception slowly separated these institutions from one another. As the nineteenth century gave way to the twentieth, new ideas about information management led to the separation of these three different institutions. According to Waibel and Erway (2009), things have now come full circle to a point of collaboration. This returning trend of LAM convergence, in theory, can better fulfill the joint mission of libraries, archives, and museums by allowing them to operate together as comprehensive memory institutions that provide a more complete and enhanced user experience.

References

Alexander, Edward Porter, and Mary Alexander. 2008. *Museums in Motion: An Introduction to the History and Functions of Museums*. 2nd ed. Lanham, MD: Altamira Press.

American Alliance of Museums. 2013. "Eligibility Criteria." http://www.aam-us.org /resources/assessment-programs/accreditation/eligibility.

Bates, M. J. 1999. "The Invisible Substrate of Information Science." *Journal of the American Society for Information Science* 50, no. 12: 1043–1050.

Bates, M. J. 2012. "The Information Professions: Knowledge, Memory, Heritage." Paper presented at Association for Library and Science Education conference, Dallas, Texas, January 18.

Buck, Rebecca A., and Jean Allman Gilmore. 2010. *MRM5: Museum Registration Methods*. 5th ed. Washington, DC: American Association of Museums Press.

Canadian Museums Association. 2013. "Museums Are. . . ." http://www.museums.ca.

Desvallées, André, and François Mairesse, eds. 2010. *Key Concepts of Museology*. Paris: Armand Colin and ICOM.

Duff, Wendy M., and Joan M. Cherry. 2000. "Use of Historical Documents in a Digital World: Comparisons with Original Materials and Microfiche." *Information Research* 6, no. 1.

Falk, John H., and Lynn D. Dierking. 1992. *The Museum Experience*. Washington, DC: Whalesback Books.

Falk, John H., and Lynn D. Dierking. 2000. *Learning from Museums: Visitor Experiences and the Making of Meaning*. Walnut Creek, CA: Altamira Press.

Given, Lisa M., and Lianne McTavish. 2010. "What's Old Is New Again: The Reconvergence of Libraries, Archives, and Museums in the Digital Age." *Library Quarterly* 80, no. 1: 7–32.

Google Art Project. n.d. http://www.google.com/culturalinstitute/project/art-project.

Gopnik, Adam. 2007. "The Mindful Museum." https://www.byliner.com/adam-gopnik/ stories/the-mindful-museum.

Hooper-Greenhill, Eilean. 1992. *Museums and the Shaping of Knowledge*. New York: Routledge.

ICOM. n.d. "Museum Definition." http://icom.museum/the-vision/museum-definition.

Keene, Suzanne. 2002. *Managing Conservation in Museums*. 2nd ed. Oxford: Butterworth-Heinemann.

Latham, Kiersten F. 2009. "Numinous Experiences with Museum Objects." Diss., School of Library and Information Management, Emporia State University.

Latham, Kiersten F. 2013. "Numinous Experiences with Museum Objects." *Visitor Studies* 16, no. 1: 3-20.

Latham, Kiersten F. 2014. "Project Real Thing." Unpublished manuscript.

Lewis, Geoffrey D. n.d. "History of Museums." *Encyclopedia Britannica*. http://www .britannica.com/EBchecked/topic/398827/history-of-museums.

Macey, David. 2000. *Dictionary of Critical Theory*. London: Penguin Books.

MacLeod, Suzanne. 2001. "Making Museum Studies: Training, Education, Research and Practice." *Museum Management and Curatorship* 19, no. 1: 51–61.

Malaro, Marie C., and Ildiko DeAngelis. 2012. *A Legal Primer on Managing Museum Collections*. 3rd ed. Washington, DC: Smithsonian Books.

Maroević, Ivo. 1998. *Introduction to Museology: The European Approach*. Munich: C. Müller-Straten.

Maroević, Ivo. 2000. "Museology as a Field of Knowledge." *ICOM International Committee for Museology Study Series* 8: 5–7.

Marstine, Janet. 2006. *New Museum Theory and Practice: An Introduction*. Malden, MA: Wiley-Blackwell.

Moore, Kevin. 1997. *Museums and Popular Culture*. London: Leicester University Press.

Museum Services Act. 1976. 20 U.S.C. § 968(4).

Museums Association. 2013. "What Is a Museum?" http://www.museumsassociation .org/about/frequently-asked-questions.

Phelan, Marilyn E. 2014. *Museum Law. A Guide for Officers, Directors and Counsel*. 4th ed. Lanham, MD: Rowman and Littlefield.

Reach Advisors. 2010. "Museum Audience Insight." http://reachadvisors.typepad.com.

Rounds, Jay. 2001. "Is There a Core Literature in Museology?" *Curator: The Museum Journal* 44, no. 2: 194–206.

Sandys, George. 1615. *A Relation of a Journey begun An. Dom. 1610. Foure Bookes. Containing a Description of the Turkish Empire, of Aegypt, of the Holy Land, of the Remote Parts of Italy, and Ilands Adjoying*. London: W. Barrett.

Simmons, John E. 2006. "Museum Studies Programs in North America." In *Museum Studies: Perspectives and Innovations*, edited by Stephen L. Williams and Catharine A. Hawks, 113–128. Washington, DC: Society for the Preservation of Natural History Collections.

Simmons, John E. 2010. "History of Museums." In *Encyclopedia of Library and Information Sciences*, edited by Marcia J. Bates and Mary Niles Maack, 2096–2106. New York: Taylor and Francis.

Teather, J. Lynne. 1991. "Museum Studies: Reflecting on Reflective Practice." *Museum Management and Curatorship* 10, no. 4: 403–417.

Van Mensch, P. 1992. "Towards a Methodology of Museology." PhD diss., University of Zagreb.

Waibel, Günter, and Ricky Erway. 2009. "Think Global, Act Local—Library, Archive and Museum Collaboration." *Museum Management and Curatorship* 24, no. 4: 323–335.

Williams, Stephen L., and Catharine A. Hawks. 2006. *Museum Studies: Perspectives and Innovations*. Washington, DC: Society for the Preservation of Natural History Collections.

Zorich, Diane, Günter Waibel, and Ricky Erway. 2008. *Beyond the Silos of the LAMs: Collaboration Among Libraries, Archives and Museums*. Dublin: OCLC Research. http://www.oclc.org/resources/research/publications/library/2008/2008 -05.pdf.

2

The Origins of Museums

A Brief History of Museums and Collections

Museums developed in response to the human need to understand the world. Collecting objects is a near-universal human trait, with collection-making found in a diverse array of human cultures. For example, archaeological evidence indicates that Neanderthals collected tools, worked shells and other objects, and carefully arranged them in their burial sites, and a 4,000-year-old Bronze Age grave in England included a collection of fossil sea urchins. The accumulation, organization, and interpretation of objects are all ways that humans make sense of the chaotic world around them. Making connections between objects is a way of finding order, a fundamental step in learning and understanding one's world. As Stephen Jay Gould (Gould and Purcell 1987) has argued, the way people classify objects is a reflection of human thought, and the study of classification assists in understanding the history of human perception.

Simply accumulating objects is different from collecting them. What distinguishes a collection from an assemblage is that collections are made for a purpose, while assemblages occur by chance. All collections have some sort of order, even though the order may be comprehensible only to the collectors. Because collections are gathered with intention, the history of collecting can reveal much about the evolution of the perception and use of objects over time. However, as Eileen Hooper-Greenhill (1992) argues in *Museums and the Shaping of Knowledge*, the history of museums cannot be understood as a linear trajectory of development, because collectors have had different motivations and directions at different times, with the result that collections themselves have historically specific natures. As discussed in more detail below, although many aspects of the early history of museums are obscure, the making of personal collections is a very old practice.

In European cultures the accumulation of personal collections that began in antiquity continued through the late Middle Ages and into the Renaissance. During this time some individuals amassed impressive collections that they used to demonstrate their wealth and power; other personal collections became the property of religious institutions. At the end of the Renaissance some of these personal collections became the property of the state, which ultimately led to collections that became increasingly more accessible to the public. Following the Renaissance, particularly during the Enlightenment, many of the state-owned collections evolved into modern museums.

Collections in the Ancient World

People made collections long before there were museums to put them in. This distinction is important because a collection can exist without a museum, but museums cannot exist without objects. In fact, many of the activities that define today's museums can be found before the first museum institutions existed. Developing and exhibiting collections, as well as preserving objects in collections, all occurred in the precursors to museums.

Europe is often credited as being the cradle of museums, although the earliest known collecting traditions developed in antiquity in Africa, Arabia, and Asia. The oldest identified example of a documented collection of objects is from the ancient Sumerian city of Ur of the Chaldees (located in present-day Iraq). Archaeological excavations by C. L. Woolsey and others in the early 1900s unearthed a collection of antiquities that dates to around 530 BC. Some of the objects in the collection were associated with clay tablets that served as object labels, recording where the objects were from, who had found them, and who had collected them. Some other very early examples are

- an extensive collection of more than 20,000 clay tablets written in cuneiform script that were accumulated in the state archives at Ebla, about 2250 BC;
- collections of inscriptions from the second millennium in Mesopotamia, used to teach scribes how to make records (an early example of the association of objects and learning);
- art, antiquities, flora, and fauna from Asia collected by Tuthmosis III (1481–1425 BC) of Egypt;
- a fossil sea urchin in a collection made around 2500 BC in Heliopolis, Egypt, inscribed with hieroglyphs giving the name of its collector and the location where it was found;
- gold and bronze artifacts collected during the Shang dynasty (ca. 1600–1025 BC) in China; and
- large private collections of the Babylonian kings Nebuchadnezzar (ca. 634–562 BC) and Nabonidus (ca. 620–539 BC), which included art objects, antiquities, and probably natural history specimens.

The exhibition of objects also began before the appearance of the modern museum. Art collections in ancient Greece took the form of exhibitions of paintings and sculptures in the entrance peristyles and porches of temples, in areas known as *pinakotheke*, or picture galleries. Wealthy Roman citizens collected paintings and other objects that were considered unusual, including fossils, and exhibited them in their homes. Several private collections of exotic seashells were found during the excavation of the ruins of Pompeii, preserved when the city was buried in volcanic ash from Mount Vesuvius in AD 79. These sorts of collections—of fossils, precious stones, decorative objects, and antiquities—have been found in numerous ancient Greek and Roman cities, revealing the extent of this activity. Although the interpretation of objects is closely related to their exhibition, very little is known about how the actual objects in these early collections were interpreted.

The preservation of collection objects was also a concern in the ancient world. For example, the Egyptians used cedar oil and dried chrysanthemums (which contain pyrethrums, a natural pest repellant) to protect mummies from pests; the ancient Chinese used camphor extracted from tree sap inside scroll boxes in the royal archives to preserve written documents; and organic objects were dehydrated and sometimes coated with wax or varnish for preservation. In the *Odyssey*, Homer mentions the practice of burning sulfur to fumigate buildings.

The Origin of the Word *Museum*

The modern concept of the museum has its roots in antiquity in the Temple of the Muses, a place that embodied the concept of learning from objects. The temple flourished in Alexandria from around 330 to 30 BC. As mentioned in Chapter 1, the word *museum* is derived from the Greek *mouseion*, meaning seat of the muses, the Greek sister-goddesses (see Table 2.1) who were the personification of knowledge in various areas and said to inspire artists, poets, philosophers, and others.

The Temple of the Muses was founded by the ruler of Alexandria, Ptolemy Sotor (305–283 BC), and the collections are reported to have included objects of art and natural history, a zoo, and a botanical garden, along with the largest library in the ancient world (Empereur 2002). The temple was an important center of Hellenistic intellectual life, and many significant thinkers were associated with it. For example, Euclid (325–265 BC) lived in Alexandria when he invented geometry; the first steam-powered device was invented by Hero (ca. AD 10–70) when he taught at the temple; the first map to use latitudinal and longitudinal lines was drawn in Alexandria by Claudius Ptolemy (ca. AD 90–168); and the first accurate estimate of the circumference of the earth was made in Alexandria by Eratosthenes (276–195 BC). Unfortunately, the Temple of the Muses was destroyed in a large fire that swept through Alexandria around 48 BC. Although the Temple was more like a modern university than a modern museum, it is important because it represents the early association of objects (including texts) with learning. When the word *museum* was later used to describe the collections of the Medici family of Florence, it was in recognition of the importance of objects in the accumulation of knowledge and the encyclopedic scope of the Medici collections, as seen in the Temple of the Muses.

Table 2.1 The Muses

Name of the Muse	Area of Influence
Clio	History
Euterpe	Music
Thalia	Comedy
Melpomene	Tragedy
Terpsichore	Dance and choral song
Erato	Lyric and love poetry
Polyhymnia	Sacred song
Urania	Astronomy
Calliope	Epic poetry

Collections during Medieval Times

In Europe following the collapse of the Roman Empire, many personal collections became the property of the church, which was then the most powerful and influential institution in society and the center of intellectual activity. In addition, travelers returning from the Holy Land often brought back objects that were exhibited in churches, including art objects and religious relics as well as nonsacred objects, classical statuary, and historical artifacts. For example, Henry of Blois (1099–1171), the bishop of Winchester and the abbot of Glastonbury, brought a collection of classical statuary back from Rome in 1151 that was then exhibited in his church. Some of the church collections were quite fantastic: the Milan cathedral boasted a hair from the beard of Noah; the Halberstadt cathedral exhibited a bone from the whale that swallowed Jonah; and the Brunswick cathedral collection included a griffin's claw, brought back from Palestine by Duke Henry the Lion. Such objects were accepted in the church collections because they were unusual and because it was believed they were evidence of a divine presence in the world. Consider a popular object during this period, ostrich eggs—at a time when very few Europeans had seen an ostrich or an illustration of an ostrich, these unusually large eggs were sometimes believed to be eggs of the mythical griffin, but at other times ostrich eggs were accepted as proof of the creatures that were mentioned in the biblical book of Job.

In the Middle East a period of intense intellectual activity took place between about AD 900 and 1200 that led to the translation of many classical Greek texts into Arabic and to the development of extensive archives and collections of artistic works. During this time a collecting tradition was formalized based on the Islamic concept of property, *waqf* (Lewis 1992), that was given for the public good. There is a long tradition of pilgrims bringing gifts to be exhibited at the shrine of Imam Aliar-Rida at Meshed (in what is now northeast Iran). Collections were also accumulated as the spoils of war, such as the works of art, textiles, weapons, and glass objects obtained by the Abbasid caliphs of Baghdad following their defeat of the Umayyad caliphs of Damascus in the middle of the eighth century.

The work of the Arabic scholars and translators reached Europe during the twelfth and thirteenth centuries when the Arabic translations of Greek texts were translated into Latin, initiating an admiration for the works of classical antiquity in Europe, which in turn played an important part in bringing about the Renaissance in Europe.

Collections in the Renaissance

The intellectual curiosity of Renaissance scholars and royalty stimulated the growth of personal collections in Europe. It was in this period from the fourteenth to the seventeenth centuries that the first cabinets of curiosities (also called *kunstkammer, wunderkammer, cabinets de curieux*, and *studioli*) appeared in Europe. Wealthy citizens, members of royal families, lawyers, physicians, and apothecaries privately owned the cabinets of curiosities. The name comes from the fact that the collections originally were housed in cabinets—pieces of furniture—but many grew to occupy entire rooms or suites of rooms. The collections in the cabinets varied by owner, but often included objects interpreted as unicorn horns, giants' bones, griffins' claws, and giant snake tongues, along with jewels, coins, maps and manuscripts, religious relics, classical art, statuary, and the occasional artifact from Asia or Africa. Many of the objects were highly prized for their alchemical properties, such as healing stones and mummy dust. From contemporary descriptions and depictions and from studies of surviving collections, it is now known that unicorn horns were really narwhal tusks, the bones of giants were from elephants or mastodons, goat and antelope horns were thought to be griffins' claws, and fossil sharks' teeth were taken for giant snake tongues. Some of the cabinets of curiosities were made to demonstrate the prestige of the owners, but others were formed with scholarly purposes. For example, the cabinet of curiosities of Ferrante Imperato (ca. 1525–1615), an apothecary in Naples, included specimens that he used in conjunction with his library for teaching purposes and that formed the basis for his 1599 book, *Dell'Historia Naturale*; the cabinet assembled by Ulisse Aldrovandi (1522–1605), a professor at the University of Bologna, contained artifacts and natural history specimens used in teaching.

REALITY CHECK

Witnessing the Past

While in Italy teaching my course Museum Origins, I made a day trip to Bologna to see the Aldrovandi collection. Ulisse Aldrovandi is known by some as the founder of modern natural history. Housed in the same university where he started the collection, this "theater" or "microcosm of nature" was a highlight of all my visits to Italy. Imagine wandering the same campus (often named as the first university in the world) where Aldrovandi assembled one of the first collections for the distinct purpose of study (in a university setting). Aldrovandi believed that firsthand observation, seeing "the things of nature," was indispensable for research and teaching. In a rich period of discovery—the sixteenth century—he brought the world to Bologna by collecting and preserving natural things from Italy and beyond. And there I stood among the objects used during this amazing period in the history of museums. I suppose one of the things that makes this collection so special to me is that Aldrovandi truly appreciated the value of seeing the actual objects in order to teach and learn from them. (KFL)

Although the collections in many of the cabinets may seem to be random and disconnected objects, in fact they reflected their owners' notions of art, nature, and divinity, and the idea that nature was formulated by divine agency. The use of symbols and allegory in the cabinets permitted the representation in miniature of the universe in the form of the collection (sometimes called a memory theater), while a theory of the innate meaning of objects determined their relationships. To the Renaissance collectors, their collections of objects were a microcosm of the universe that pointed to the divinely sanctioned, ideal order of the world. What collectors wanted were not ordinary, common objects, but objects that were rare or exotic and could be interpreted as evidence of a divine presence in the world, as well as show the owner's magnificence in owning such rare items.

Collections such as those of the Medici were used for study by their owners and displayed to family members, friends, and visitors. Much of what is known about the objects in the cabinets and their arrangements (classification) comes from contemporary depictions in drawings, prints, and paintings. Susan Pearce (1992), an expert on collecting, has pointed out that the collecting of objects is a complex material practice and that a collection is steeped in ideology and function; collections are a form of creation of a self-identity that reinforces or undermines the dominant categories of the society in which the collection appears. As did the collections in the Temple of the Muses, the cabinets served as information resources to enlighten viewers about the meaning of the world around them, but also to aid in the owner's self-identity.

During the Renaissance the belief in the power of objects greatly influenced what was sought after and preserved. The collections in the Medici palace in Florence, for example, were intended to show off the wealth and power of the Medici family by using the past to glorify the current family members. By possessing objects that were believed to have great power, the Medici family showed that it, too, had great power (Hooper-Greenhill 1992). The Medici collections were officially opened to the public at the Uffizi Palace in 1582 and ultimately were bequeathed to the state of Tuscany in 1743. Similarly, between 1523 and 1582 another well-known Renaissance family, the Grimani family, donated most of their collections to the Venetian Republic, and many of these objects can now be found in the Museo d'Antichità, in the Doge's Palace in Venice.

REALITY CHECK

Witnessing the Past: The Medici and the Origin of Museums

During the summer I teach a course in Florence, Italy, on the origins of museums. During my first full class on-site in Florence, I found myself completely fascinated with the Medici family (as did my students) and truly understood the extent to which they have influenced museums around the world. Many of the political, propagandistic, and personal choices that members of this family made have come to affect the modern museum in significant ways, most especially their belief in the power of objects as representations of power and knowledge. In fact, once you become aware of the Medici influence, you would be surprised how often they are still mentioned, not only in museal contexts, but in many other daily activities and institutions across the world. This one family, beginning with Cosimo the Elder in the fifteenth century, helped set the stage for many museum activities and processes that we have come to take for granted in museums, such as collecting systematically, exhibiting objects, inventorying collections, and interpreting the meaning of objects to visitors. (KFL)

Early Classification Schemes and Catalogs

As objects amassed in the private cabinets of curiosities in Europe from about the 1400s on, classification schemes were needed to give order to the objects. Initially objects were simply perceived as *mirabilia* (finite marvels) and *miracula* (infinite or divine marvels), or *artificialia* and *naturalia*. As the collections grew larger and more complex, new categories were added, such as *antiquitas* for objects of historical import. The contents of the cabinets were highly varied. The philosopher Francis Bacon (1561–1626) described a typical cabinet of curiosities as containing "whatsoever the hand of man by exquisite art or engine has made rare in stuff, form, or motion; whatsoever singularity, chance and the shuffle of things hath produced; whatsoever Nature has wrought in things that want life and may be kept" (Bacon 1594). The diversity of objects in the collections of the cabinets and the attempts at classification seemed to confirm the existence of a divine being and demonstrated to their collectors that there was a divine order in nature.

The first museum catalogs, which were handwritten, were little more than descriptive inventories of collections, but rapidly evolved into detailed listings of museum contents, often with illustrations and histories of important objects after the introduction of printing with moveable type. Ulisse Aldrovandi (1522–1605) went so far with his museum cataloging as to also produce a *Catalogus virorum qui vistarunt Musaeum nostrum*, in which he categorized his visitors according to their geographical origins and social standing.

One of the first printed books about museums was written by Samuel von Quiccheberg (1529–1567), a physician in Antwerp, and published in Munich in 1565. Von Quiccheberg's book was titled *Vel Tituli Theatri Amplissimi* (Inscriptions of the immense theater); it was written in German despite its Latin title. Von Quiccheberg wrote that a collection should be a systematic classification of the materials of the universe, and he provided guidelines for assembling what he considered to be an ideal cabinet of curiosities, proposing an organizational scheme that classified objects into groups that correlate with modern museum divisions: material glorifying the founder and handcrafts from antiquity (historic objects), natural specimens (natural history materials), technical and cultural objects (applied art and crafts), and paintings and sacred objects (fine art). Von Quiccheberg perceived the collections as objects to be studied to gain knowledge and provoke a sense of wonder.

The collection compiled by Olaus Worm (1588–1654) in Copenhagen beginning in 1620 was described in an extensive catalog, *Museum Wormianum*, published in 1655. Worm's catalog included a woodcut depicting the main room of Worm's museum that has been widely reproduced in publications about museums (see Figure 2.1).

Figure 2.1   The Museum Olaus Worm.

The Enlightenment and the Birth of the Modern European Museum

As the Renaissance gave way to the Enlightenment, beginning around 1650 the collections that had begun as cabinets of curiosities grew larger and became better known through the circulation of catalogs. As knowledge of the world beyond Europe spread, the objects that were collected gradually shifted from the unusual to the typical and usual, which changed the nature of the collections in profound ways. In the atmosphere of the Enlightenment the study of objects evolved as a way to understand the unknown. Objects arriving in Europe from Africa, the Americas, Asia, and Australia became valued for the information they carried about unknown territories. This was an era when systems and scientific methods were being applied to understand both human culture and nature. For example, Francis Bacon (1561–1626) argued for the application of inductive empiricism to the cataloging of knowledge, and René Descartes (1596–1650) sought to rationalize science and religion, developments that were reflected in the evolution of museum collections. In his study of the development of museums in the United States, Joel Orosz (1990) noted that during the Enlightenment, objects took on a new importance as collections were recognized as preserving works of art, historical artifacts, and natural history specimens that served as the evidence required to substantiate the claims of scholarly reason.

An example of a collection that grew from a cabinet of curiosities into a modern museum is that of John Tradescant the Elder (ca. 1570–1638) and his son, John Tradescant the Younger (1608–1662), in England. The Tradescants' extensive collection included natural history specimens, precious stones, weapons, coins, carvings, paintings, and medallions, which were exhibited to the public for a fee. As their collection grew, the Tradescants sought the services of Elias Ashmole (1617–1692) to catalog it. Ashmole's catalog of the collection was published in 1656 under the title *Musaeum Tradescantianum*. After the death of both Tradescants, Ashmole gained control of the collection and donated it to Oxford University, renaming it after himself (Swann 2001). After its opening in 1683, the Ashmolean Museum established the pattern for what eventually became the modern university museum, with space for exhibition and storage of collections as well as offices for the teaching staff associated with the university.

Modern Museums

Museums were numerous enough in Europe after 1700 that a museum object dealer from Hamburg named Caspar Neikelius (a pseudonym for Kaspar Freidrich Jenequel) published a book called *Museographica* (1727), considered to be the first museologically focused work. Neikelius provided guidance for acquisitions; addressed problems of classification of the objects in the collection; presented techniques for caring for collections; and suggested putting a table in the middle of each room, "where things brought from the repository could be studied." He also recommended that museum objects be stored in dry conditions and kept out of direct sunlight, and that museums should have an accession book and a general catalog. Neikelius was the first to articulate the difference between viewing objects clustered in a small room (e.g., as in a cabinet of curiosities) and those displayed in a long room (an exhibition hall derived from the *grande salle* of French medieval chateaux). In 1753 David Hultman published his recommendations for museums, stating that a museum building should be made of brick, be longer than it is wide, and have windows facing north to provide indirect sunlight.

As museums grew larger and more complex in the eighteenth century, they began to diverge into specialized institutions (e.g., art, ethnographic, history, military, natural history, technology), based on the characteristics of their collections and the systems of order used to categorize the objects in their collection. For example, natural history collections were influenced greatly by the advent of new taxonomic classification systems for plants (in 1735) and animals (in 1758) developed by the Swedish naturalist, Carl Linnaeus (1707–1778). This efficient, modern classification system quickly became the principle around which natural history collections were organized and collection growth was directed. An equivalent common universal cataloging taxonomy for human-made objects did not become available until 1978. By contrast, the Dewey Decimal system for the cataloging of library materials in ten major classes first appeared in 1876, the Library of Congress system (using twenty-one classes) was first published in 1897, and the Universal Decimal Classification was published in Europe in 1895.

The Continuing Development of the European Modern Museum: Eighteenth and Nineteenth Centuries

The development of mercantilism, the rise of an affluent merchant class, and the decline of royal patronage systems together led to a greater public interest in the arts beginning early in the eighteenth century. By the middle of the eighteenth century, the dawning Industrial Revolution sparked public interest in technology and science. At the beginning of the nineteenth century, as people realized that museums could contribute to the formation of national consciousness, came the recognition that the museum was the appropriate institution for the preservation of a nation's history and heritage, which brought about a period of museum-building in Europe. So much museum growth occurred during this time that the nineteenth century has been called "The Golden Age of Museums," because nearly every country in Western Europe opened a comprehensive museum during this time. Many of the new modern museums were less encyclopedic than their precursors and more focused in their collections, such as the first of what are now the Vatican Museums, the Museo Sacro, which opened in Rome in 1756. A number of museums specializing in art, history, and natural history were also founded at this time. In 1773 Pope Clement XIV opened the first museum devoted exclusively to art, the Pio Clemente Museum in Rome (the museum's holdings are now part of the Vatican collections); in the same year the Louvre in Paris began to admit public visitors to the collections.

Most early European museums started with collections assembled by happenstance, but some were planned more thoroughly. For example, the first modern art museum was the Hermitage in St. Petersburg, Russia, which was established in 1764; the Czartoryski Museum (Krakow) was founded in 1776 to make collections from the aristocracy accessible to the general public. Several museums in this period established standards that still affect museum practice, such as the suggestion in 1779 by Christian Von Mechel that the Belvedere Museum in Vienna be arranged to present "a visible history of art," in a chronological framework, which was followed by the Altes Museum in Berlin (1830), also designed to show a chronological history of art. The Alte Pinakothek (a reference to the Greek concept of objects assembled for use in teaching) in Munich (1836) went a step further and opened with a chronological exhibit of art organized by schools, with gallery spaces designed to protect the artwork from fire, dust, and vibration, with north-facing windows and moderate heat in the winter.

A number of significant museums were founded in the late 1700s and early 1800s. The British Museum was opened to the public in 1759 (with free admission), with its collections of art, anthropology, history, science, and a library, making it a universal institution. Charles III of Spain brought together works of art and natural history in 1785 as a museum of natural science, which eventually became the Prado in 1819. The Louvre opened to the public as the Musée Central des Artes in Paris in 1793, shortly after the French Revolution, exhibiting royal collections that had previously been unavailable to the public, outside of an occasional special exhibition. The new French museum grew rapidly as Napoleon appropriated objects for the collections during his European campaigns (most of this material was later repatriated, after the Congress of Vienna in 1815).

The first ethnology museum opened in Leiden in 1837. Historic house museums first appeared in the mid-nineteenth century in Europe and the United States, dedicated to preserving buildings because of their significant architecture or association with a significant person or historical event. Open-air museums or living museums, which usually include period architecture and historical reenactors, were first developed in the late nineteenth century in Scandinavia; the first one opened in 1881 near Oslo, Norway, to exhibit the collections of King Oscar II. In 1891 Arthur Hazelius founded the Skansen museum in Stockholm, Sweden, which became the model for subsequent open-air museums around the world. And the first mobile museum was developed in Liverpool, England, in 1884 to serve schoolchildren.

In the latter part of the nineteenth century museums were recast as primarily educational institutions as the "new museum idea"—the separation of study collections from exhibition collections—took hold. Sir William Henry Flower, director of the British Museum, formally articulated the new museum idea by proposing that museums be organized around the dual purposes of research and public education. Until this time, museums had been expected to put all of their collections on display, with the result that exhibit halls were often vast arrays of carefully labeled and arranged objects in ordered cases. Although it has become fashionable to criticize this style of exhibit, it was very popular with visitors who sought out museums to see things that they had never seen before, arranged in a way that made sense of the chaos around them. The second half of the nineteenth century was also the first period of major growth in museums, with more than one hundred new museums opening in the United Kingdom and at least fifty new museums in Germany, and many significant museums opening in the Americas.

Museums in the Americas

The Enlightenment idea of the modern museum became established in the American colonies in the late eighteenth century. The Charleston (South Carolina) Library Society started the first museum in the United States (the society's collections were later moved to the College of Charleston). In 1785 Charles Willson Peale (1741–1827) founded in his home in Philadelphia the first museum regularly open to the public in the United States. Based on the European concept of a museum, Peale's innovation was his democratic intention to provide instruction and entertainment to all classes of people (provided they paid the entrance fee). Peale's museum included paintings by himself and his sons, taxidermy mounts, fossils, a mastodon skeleton, ethnographic objects, and live animals. The museum eventually failed when it was confronted with many of the same problems that many museums face today: lack of funding, insufficient audience, and a presentation of the collection that failed to bring in repeat visitors. The Peale collections were dispersed at auction in 1858.

Another influential museum pioneer in the United States was Phineas T. Barnum (1810–1891), later to become the well-known circus magnate, who opened a huge public museum called The American Museum in New York City. The museum had been founded by the Tammany Society in 1790 and purchased by John Scudder (1775–1821) in 1802, who operated it as Scudder's American Museum. Barnum purchased the collection from Scudder in 1841 and operated it as The American Museum until 1865, when it burned down. In his museum Barnum exhibited more than 600,000 objects, but he finally gave up on museums and went into the circus business after more disastrous museum fires.

Although two significant American museums were founded in 1870—the Metropolitan Museum in New York and the Museum of Fine Arts in Boston—only 4 percent of museums known today in the United States were in existence before 1900. At least 75 percent of today's museums in the United States were founded after 1950, and 40 percent were founded after 1970.

The first outdoor museums in the United States were the historic environments known as Colonial Williamsburg, established in 1926, and Henry Ford's Greenfield Village, which opened in Dearborn, Michigan, in 1929. Founded in 1850 in Newburgh, New York, the first historic house museum in the United States was Hasbrouck House, once the headquarters of General George Washington.

The mid- to late nineteenth century was a time for museum growth in much of the Western world. The first museum in Latin America, the Museo de Historia Natural in Mexico City, was founded in 1790, followed by the Museo de Historia Natural in Buenos Aires in 1812, with national museums being founded in most of the other Latin American countries before the end of the nineteenth century.

During the twentieth century museums in the Americas (and in several other regions), particularly in the United States, prospered and diversified into the variety of museums seen today, including children's museums, commercial museums, science centers, community and regional museums, and specialty museums, as discussed in Chapter 5.

Non-Western Museums: Beyond Colonialism

Although the idea of the modern public museum is essentially European in origin, it was successfully exported to other parts of the world through trade and colonialism. There was a great period of growth in Asian museums in the 1800s and in African museums in the early 1900s (e.g., national museums were founded in what is now Zimbabwe in 1901 and in Uganda in 1908). Many colonial-era museums have evolved into important national museums, particularly in South America and Asia. For example, the Asiatic Society of Bengal opened a museum in 1814 in Calcutta, India, that became a national museum following the independence of India in 1947, and the first museum in Africa was the South African Museum, founded in Cape Town in 1825. As independent nations emerged from their colonial roots, some museums became important agencies for developing national identity by offering interpretations of their collections that reflected feelings of national ownership (e.g., defined national culture), as well as defined nationality compared to other nations and cultures.

Some of these museums played a significant role in the rejection of colonialism. For example, during the 1970s many Caribbean museums shifted their emphasis from a strong focus on their society's colonial past to present more inclusive cultural and natural histories. The last decade has seen a growth in what are called "museos de memoria" (museums of memory), institutions dedicated to bringing closure to such events as civil wars, violent political oppression, and prolonged periods of prejudice.

The Importance of Roots

Museums, libraries, and archives share a common past. As discussed earlier in this chapter, some of the oldest collections in the world were clay tablets written in the second and third millennia in cuneiform and other scripts. Tablets remaining from these early archives have been found by archaeologists at Ebla and Mari (in modern-day Syria), Amarna (Egypt), Hathusa (Turkey), and Pylos (Greece). The ancient Babylonians, Chinese, and Romans also kept archival and library collections, and the institution that gave us the concept of the museum (the Temple of the Muses in Alexandria) included the largest library in the ancient world. It was largely the translation of textual materials by the Arabs during the period AD 900 to 1200 that stimulated the Renaissance in Europe and led to the development of modern museums, libraries, and archives. The development of libraries and museums is also closely linked to the introduction of printing with moveable type in Europe around 1450 and the rise of universities during the 1600s, as exemplified by the Bodleian library at Oxford University and the library of the British Museum. The introduction of printing made it possible for museums to circulate their catalogs and thus gain a wider audience for their collections. History shows that museums, along with archives and libraries, have evolved to serve different needs at different times, but have always played a significant role in interpreting nature and culture. Museums will continue to serve a significant role in society as long as humans remain curious about the world around them.

References

Alderson, William T. 1992. *Mermaids, Mummies, and Mastodons: The Emergence of the American Museum*. Washington, DC: American Association of Museums.

Bacon, Francis. 1594. *Gesta Grayorum, or, The History of the High and Mighty Prince, Henry Prince of Purpoole . . . Who Reigned and Died, A.D. 1594: Together with a Masque, as It Was Presented (by His Highness's Command) for the Entertainment of Q. Elizabeth, Who, with the Nobels of Both Courts, Was Present Thereat*. London: W. Canning.

Bazin, Germain. 1967. *The Museum Age*. New York: Universe Books.

Empereur, Jean-Yves. 2002. *Alexandria: Jewel of Egypt*. New York: Harry Abrams.

Findlen, Paula. 1989. "The Museum: Its Classical Etymology and Renaissance Genealogy." *Journal of the History of Collections* 1, no. 1: 59–78.

Goode, George Brown. 1889. "Museum-History and Museums of History." *Papers of the American Historical Association* 3, no. 2: 253–275.

Gould, Stephen J., and Rosamand Wolff Purcell. 1987. *Illuminations: A Bestiary*. New York: W.W. Norton.

Grew, Nehemiah. 1681. *Musaeum Regalis Societatis. Or a Catalogue and Description of the Natural and Artificial Rarities Belonging to the Royal Society and Preserved at Gresham Colledge. Made by Nehemjah Grew M.D. Fellow of the Royal*

Society, and of the Colledge of Physitians. Whereunto Is Subjoyned the Compar-ative Anatomy of Stomachs and Guts. By the Same Author. London: W. Rawlins.

Holdengräber, Paul. 1987. "'A Visible History of Art': The Forms and Preoccupations of the Early Museum." In *Studies in Eighteenth-Century Culture*, edited by John Yolton and Leslie Ellen Brown, 107–117. East Lansing, MI: Colleagues Press.

Hooper-Greenhill, Eilean. 1992. *Museums and the Shaping of Knowledge*. London: Routledge.

Impey, Oliver R., and Arthur MacGregor. 1985. *The Origins of Museums: The Cabinet of Curiosities in Sixteenth and Seventeenth Century Europe*. Oxford: Clarendon Press.

Lewis, Geoffrey D. 1992. "Museums and Their Precursors: A Brief World Survey." In *Manual of Curatorship*, 2nd ed., edited by John M. A. Thompson, 5–21. London: Butterworth-Heinemann.

Lindauer, Margaret A. 2009. "Cabinets of Curiosities." In *Encyclopedia of Library and Information Sciences,* 3rd ed., edited by Marcia J. Bates and Mary Niles Maack, 721–724. New York: Taylor and Francis.

Mauriès, Patrick. 2002. *Cabinets of Curiosities*. London: Thames and Hudson.

Murray, David. 2000. *Museums, Their History and Their Use: With a Bibliography and List of Museums in the United Kingdom*. Reprint 1904 ed. Staten Island, NY: Pober Publications.

Mayor, Adrienne. 2011. *The First Fossil Hunters: Dinosaurs, Mammoths, and Myth in Greek and Roman Times*. Princeton, NJ: Princeton University Press.

Muensterberger, Werner. 1995. *Collecting: An Unruly Passion; Psychological Per-spectives*. San Diego: Harcourt Brace and Company.

Orosz, Joel. 1990. *Curators and Culture: The Museum Movement in America, 1740–1870*. Tuscaloosa: University of Alabama Press.

Pearce, Susan M. 1992. *Museums, Objects and Collections: A Cultural Study*. Wash-ington, DC: Smithsonian Institution Press.

Simmons, John E. 2010. "History of Museums." In *Encyclopedia of Library and In-formation Sciences*, edited by Marcia J. Bates and Mary Niles Maack, 2096-2106. New York: Taylor and Francis.

Swann, Marjorie. 2001. *Curiosities and Texts: The Culture of Collecting in Early Modern England*. Philadelphia: University of Pennsylvania Press.

Tega, W. 2005. *Guide to the Museo di Palazzo Poggi: Science and Art*. 2nd ed. Bolo-gna: Editrice Compositori.

Whitehead, P. J. P. 1970. "Museums in the History of Zoology," *Museums Journal* 70, no. 2: 50–57.

Section Two
How

3

The Museum System

How Is a Museum a System?

Museums, as organizations, are complex entities. No two museums are alike—each has its own internal issues that affect how it functions—but all museums share concerns with other museums and nonprofit organizations. To understand how museums work, they must be considered in context, as part of a dynamic, ever-changing world. This chapter examines the museum system and other systems that affect it.

A system is a group of interrelated, interacting components that form a complex whole, a configuration of parts that are connected through a web of direct and indirect relationships. An open system continuously interacts with the environment; a closed system is isolated from its environment. Museums are open systems. Systems have several defining characteristics:

- Systems are composed of many parts (e.g., smaller systems nested within the larger system).
- Each component part plays a role within the larger system.
- Energy, materials, and/or information flow among the different parts of a system.
- System functions are affected if any one part of the system is removed.
- The system has to adjust to a new equilibrium if a change occurs in the way the parts are arranged.
- Systems depend on feedback to maintain equilibrium.
- Systems maintain their stability by adjusting to feedback.

Feedback refers to information about the past or present that influences the same phenomenon in the present or future as part of a cause-and-effect cycle (hence the information is said to "feed back" to itself). In other words, feedback is information that returns to its original transmitter and influences the transmitter's subsequent actions. A simple example of feedback is the way a thermostat works in a house: the thermostat senses the temperature in a room, then adjusts the output of the cooling or heating equipment to keep the house at a predetermined level of comfort. An example of how feedback might work in a *museum system* is when changes are made to how collection objects are interpreted for the public based on visitor evaluations.

Systems theory is the interdisciplinary study of systems that self-regulate through feedback loops. An example of systems theory applied to human interactions is family systems therapy (developed by Murray Bowen and Michael Kerr beginning in the 1950s), which is based on the principle that individual people cannot be understood in isolation, but must be understood as members of a family. The family forms an emotional unit that is composed of interconnected and interdependent individuals who make up the family system. Although each individual in the family acts independently, his or her actions affect other family members and are affected by other family members, who in turn are all interacting together as a family system.

Systems thinking is a way to study how systems work and how they influence each other. The traditional way to analyze an organization is from the point of view that it is composed of separate, distinct parts (e.g., departments or individuals). In systems thinking, the organization is conceptualized as consisting of many complex and dynamic nested systems that interact with each other within the larger system. An example from nature is an ecosystem—a community of plants and animals living in a particular place in nature, functioning as a very large system that is comprised of many smaller systems. Each species of plant or animal is adapted for its own way of life, yet the animals and plants in the ecosystem continuously interact with each other, either directly or indirectly. A change in one component, such as the extinction of a species, ultimately affects how all the other components interact. The larger ecosystem is the sum of all of the individual systems in the environment.

When systems theory and systems thinking are applied to museums, how components such as the management of collections, visitor services, educational programming, conservation, and museum administration all work together to make the museum function can be better understood. The individual components operate as smaller systems that together make up the larger museum system, which itself resides in a larger, complex external system.

The Holistic Museum Ecosystem

As mentioned above, the museum system can be likened to an ecosystem, which is a complex set of relationships between a community of organisms and the environment in which they live. Similar to the way that each organism is composed of systems functioning in a way that allows it to survive as part of the ecosystem, a museum also exists as a functioning entity within a larger system. Each museum has an *internal system* composed of the inner and outer museum (see Figure 3.1) that resides within a wider context called the *external system,* which is composed of the local and global environments that in turn affect the museum's internal system. The museum's internal system (the inner and outer museum) is reviewed here first, followed by the external system.

Figure 3.1   The holistic museum system model.

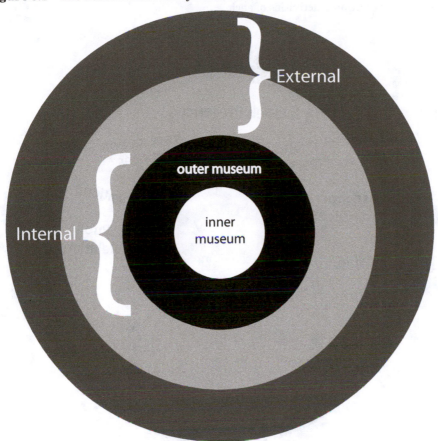

The Internal Museum System

The Inner and Outer Museum Model

Philip S. Humphrey, former director of the Natural History Museum at the University of Kansas (KU), conceptualized the museum as a two-layered, nested system comprised of an inner and an outer museum. Humphrey first described the inner museum as the collections and the people who study and care for them and the outer museum as "all those translational devices such as exhibits and public programs that make the knowledge of the inner museum available to the lay public" (Humphrey 1976). This model was probably influenced by Sir William Henry Flower's "new museum idea" in the late nineteenth century, which proposed the separation of collections into those for research and those for education. In 1991 Humphrey used the model to describe university natural history museums as an aid to understanding the unique situation and relationships within and between these museums and other nonuniversity museums.

Humphrey's model (see Figure 3.2) is useful for understanding the structure and function of the many different kinds of museums as well as a way to help shape the museum of the future. The model can be applied as a

Figure 3.2 An interpretation of Humphrey's inner and outer museum model, showing the traditional activities of each.

device to consider museum structures, functions, and relationships and to analyze the museum from many different angles. It is also very useful for understanding how museum systems work and how they have changed in recent years.

When Humphrey first developed his model in the mid-1970s, it was an adequate way to describe many museums and useful in critiquing them. In Humphrey's view, the inner museum was the hidden, working museum and the outer museum was what the public saw. However, the model was static because it situated specific activities, people, and concepts in one of two separate places. Although for a very long time museums functioned pretty much this way (and some still do today), the model positioned the view of the museum system from within rather than from a holistic viewpoint.

While there is no single structure that applies to all kinds and sizes of museums, a typical suite of departments for many museums includes administration, collections, exhibits, education, public relations, and development (see Figure 3.2). Traditionally, there was a distinct line between the inner and outer museums (e.g., a visitor would rarely have the opportunity

Figure 3.3 The museum system model (internal museum system) showing the blurred lines between the inner and outer museum.

to interact with a curator in a gallery). In recent years external structures surrounding museums have been shifting due to changes in society, technology, the economy, the increased importance placed on ways of learning and knowing, and the increased attention to community involvement in the work of the museum. These changes have altered the structures of the internal museum system. In effect, the border of the inner museum has become more permeable, allowing for more interchange with the outer museum (see Figure 3.3). Activities and job assignments tend to blend and to flow into each other as the old departmental structures dissolve, with the result that it is often difficult to identify museum functions as purely inner museum or outer museum. Even more important, the border line that used to mark the outside of the outer museum—between the museum and the external world—is now very porous, allowing ideas and information to flow between the museum and its public more than ever before. These changes show that many museums are becoming more transparent, recognizing their relationship as co-owners with the public and responding more fully to feedback. A few museums are attempting to fully implement this sort of model, dissolving the border between inner and outer museum. As a result, today it is not uncommon to see, for example, a curator interacting with visitors in the museum galleries.

The Environment (External Systems)

Ecosystems are not static—the organisms that comprise an ecosystem constantly have to adapt to change. For example, unusual periods of drought, fluctuations in the numbers of predators or prey, disease, floods, and fires affect different plants and animals in different ways. As the organisms adapt to change, there is short-term disruption in the balanced relationships between them until a new equilibrium in the system can be reached. Similarly, the external system surrounding the museum includes a complex world that is constantly evolving, and the museums that reside within it must change and adapt. In other words, a museum is part of a larger web of relationships; change may come from local, close-to-home sources or from larger, more grand, national or global sources.

By definition, as a system nested within a set of other systems, the museum is a relational entity (Bell 2012). Sometimes these relationships can dramatically influence the museum; at other times the effect is more subtle.

A seemingly small change can have far-reaching results, prompting adaptive reactions throughout the museum system. For example, studies of how people learn in museums have affected how museums go about interpreting their collections and presenting their interpretations to the public. Traditionally, museum exhibits were often rather linear, and label text dispensed whatever information museum experts considered important for the public to know. The trend now—based on new research data—is for exhibits to have multiple points of entry, with opportunities for visitors to read text, listen to audio, contemplate questions, interact among themselves, and make personal connections to the objects on exhibit. These changes have resulted in a merging of exhibit and education departments in some museums, greater involvement of knowledge experts in object presentation, and a greatly increased use of audience evaluation tools to make museums more responsive to their visitors' interests and needs. A better understanding of how people interact with objects has also changed how and what museums collect, how objects are cataloged, and what information and images of objects museums make available to the public. In turn, this greater access to objects and information associated with objects has allowed visitors to play a greater role in the interpretation of the collections by expressing their own ideas about them.

Some examples of the relationships between museums and external environments that affect internal museum structures and activities are considered below. How museums are positioned in society—as private or public institutions, within local and global economies, as community organizations, as memory institutions, as cultural heritage sites, as representations of identity or nationhood, or in a culture of commodity, for instance—can affect these relationships and ultimately the way museums function (see Figure 3.4). These examples reveal the extent to which museums are embedded in society, illustrating the way in which a museum acts as a system situated within another set of external systems.

Public and Private, Nonprofit and For-Profit

One layer of the museum's external environment is related to the type of organization it is. In Chapter 1, museums in the United States were

Figure 3.4   The internal system of the museum, surrounded by a selection of the external systems in which it lies.

Examples of External Systems that affect the Museum (internal) System

described as either public or private organizations. Public museums are owned and managed by a government (federal, state, or local), while private museums are managed by their members (usually through a governing board). Most private museums are nonprofit, meaning that they hold their collections in the public trust, and that any income the museum receives is applied directly to fulfilling its mission. Some private museums are for-profit institutions, which means they operate like a business—their collections are not held in the public trust, and any income the museum receives goes to the museum's owners. Within these categories, museums may vary greatly in terms of legal constraints regarding funding, policies, programming, and liability. The parameters that define each kind of museal organization affect how the organization functions, both internally and externally. In addition, politics associated with these categories influence how various aspects of the organizations are handled, valued, and structured.

Local Economy

Local economics, along with local politics, are almost always a factor for museums to consider, because most museums depend on their local economy in both direct and indirect ways. In turn, a museum may have a profound effect on its local economy. Museums attract visitors who spend money on food, hotels, and fuel, which boosts the local economy, and they employ people who live in the area and contribute to the local economy. At the same time, museums may depend on their local government to subsidize their operations or help promote their activities. By offering exhibits about local history and culture, the museum may support its community in other ways, but it can also be affected by local politics if people disagree with the museum's interpretive perspectives.

Community Organizations

Many diverse organizations serve communities in any given city, county, or state, but museums—because they hold their collections in the public trust—are more readily seen as institutions that belong to the community. The character of the museum as a local resource or a community organization and its relationship to other local organizations may play an important role in how it functions. For example, a local historical society that operates as the repository for city government archives can position itself to be an insular, club-like organization, or one that is open to everyone in the community, recognizing the stake local citizens have in the museum. Some museums serve as a resource for local organizations by hosting meetings or providing space for other uses.

Memory Institutions

Many museums serve the wider environment as memory institutions, along with libraries and archives. A memory institution is a repository of public knowledge, often related to a traumatic or emotional event (e.g., the United States Holocaust Memorial Museum in Washington, DC, or the National September 11 Memorial and Museum in New York City). These museums serve as long-term keepers of potential meaning, often in the form of physical representations of events, people, and ideas. In this context, museums act as the institutions that save cultural and natural heritage; they are the preservers of the past for the present and future and therefore sites of great trust for the public. Museums can serve as memory institutions on both local and global levels. For example, the Museo de la Memoria y los Derechos Humanos (Museum of Memory and Human Rights) in Santiago, Chile, memorializes the Chilean citizens who were tortured and killed by the regime of the dictator Augusto Pinochet between 1973 and 1990. Another example is L'Ossuaire de Douamont (the Douaumont Ossuary) in France, which memorializes the estimated 230,000 French and German soldiers who died in the Battle of Verdun in 1916. Not all memories preserved have to be emotional or traumatic, however, and museums find themselves acting as memory institutions in more routine scenarios such as local history and local nature preserves.

Cultural Heritage

Cultural heritage refers to the legacy of physical things and their associated meanings to society, as well as the parallel responsibility to care for and preserve these materials, and is closely related to the notion of the memory institution. It encompasses tangible and intangible culture and the natural environment. Cultural heritage is now part of the World Heritage movement spurred on by the United Nations Educational, Scientific and Cultural Organization (UNESCO). Cultural heritage encompasses more institutions than just museums, but it corresponds with all things museal, including structures, sites, monuments, and landscapes in addition to movable objects. Interesting issues are being raised in the analysis of this sphere of interest, such as who owns cultural heritage, what should be saved, what the impact and relevance of cultural property laws are, tourism, the role of virtuality, and more.

Identity/Nationhood

In a global context, museums are sometimes seen as being representative of nations, as purveyors of identity for a very large group of people. This is sometimes, but not always, intentional. Throughout their history, some museums have been used as instruments of social propaganda and nation-building. Enmeshed with identity (and economy), politics becomes involved, especially in this broader stratum.

As Moira Simpson (2001) has pointed out, museums can be used to define or reaffirm cultural or national identity by preserving objects and languages. For instance, in a tribal museum (such as the Osage Nation Museum and Library in Pawhuska, Oklahoma), a cultural group can take control of how it is represented to outsiders. Another example is the Museo Nacional de Antropología in Mexico City, which opened in 1963. The museum is huge: twenty-three acres of exhibit space, and if you walk past every exhibit, it is a stroll of fifteen kilometers (nearly ten miles). An analysis of the museum by Luis Gerardo Morales-Moreno (1994) concluded that the myth of Mexican origin was established in part through the symbiotic relationships among archaeology, the state, and the museum. In his analysis, the museum helped sanctify the history of the Mexican fatherland and formed a new national identity that integrated the pre-Hispanic past with the 1810–1821 War of Independence. Another example comes from the Caribbean where, in 1980 the minister of information and culture in Barbados observed that the national museum did not represent the diversity of Barbadian life because of its focus on white merchants and plantation owners, and therefore the museum failed to present the complete history of Barbados (Cummins 1994). A committee was established to improve the museum's representation of all strata and cultural groups in Barbados, starting a reform movement that spread through many Caribbean museums.

The Global Economy

The global economy usually has an indirect influence on museums—although how museums fare in society has a lot to do with how the national and global economies develop—because economic policies and principles affect museums. For example, changes in the global economy can produce a weakening of the currency of some countries relative to the currency of others, causing an imbalance in international programs for touring exhibitions or making imported archival supplies or museum literature unaffordable. Or a downturn in the global economy may cause an increase in unemployment or underemployment in some countries, leading to an increase in the illegal exportation of objects of cultural heritage to countries with greater wealth.

Commoditization

Any discussion of the larger contextual environment surrounding museums would not be complete without discussing the role of commoditization. A commodity is something that has both use value and exchange value (Kopytoff 1986). In the West, monetary value is taken to be the indicator of commodity status. Of late, the public perception of the value of museum objects has shifted from their being priceless to their having an ascribed monetary value that demonstrates their worth to society (e.g., it is common to see news reports of a record-setting sale price for a particular painting or object). For example, on the *Antiques Roadshow* and similar television programs, the higher the price put on an object, the more excited, impressed, and pleased the owner becomes. This commoditization of culture has been extended to tourism, a major part of which involves museums. An excellent example of commoditization of culture and museums can be found in Florence, Italy. The heart of old Florence—slightly more than 1.5 square miles—has been called one large museum. When walking around old Florence, evidence of the past is visible everywhere, from the buildings to the streets to the art that is found on every corner. Florence, as a city, has become a major tourist destination, and in the summer locals are said to flee the city center to escape the hordes of tourists (which can be in the millions, in a city of about 350,000). There is a tension between the Renaissance Florence of the past—to which the tourists flock—and the commoditization of that history in the form of knick-knacks, knock-off art, and cheap T-shirts. One can (pay to) see Michelangelo's *David* and walk just outside the museum doors to purchase a pair of boxer shorts with an image of David's pelvic region expertly printed on the front. Much of the commoditization of culture is not this obvious, but in most museums evidence of it can be found in the form of commerce in trinkets, food, posters, books, and replicas. The mind-set of commoditization greatly affects museums in a multitude of ways, for example by emphasizing the market value of an object instead of its documentary or aesthetic value, seeing collections as assets that may be converted to cash rather than as the core resources that the museum should care for and interpret, or designing exhibitions and program activities based on the amount of money they will bring in rather than their role in fulfilling the museum's mission.

Organic Networks: Relationships

Keene's (2002) definition of *museum* as "a system to build and permanently maintain an irreplaceable and meaningful physical resource and use it to transmit ideas and concepts to the public" highlights a dynamism in the system; the museum is a structure enmeshed in cycles, feedback loops, and networks. In the museum system, the relationships between the parts and with other external systems are the most important structures to understand. Becoming aware of these relationships helps clarify how all the parts are interconnected (see Figure 3.5).

No matter what part of the museum system is considered, the relationship between people and objects is at the heart of the concept of the museum. Whether considering museum workers, visitors, or nonvisitors, it comes down to human beings and their relationships with museum objects.

An object in a museum has many different uses, purposes, meanings, and experiences associated with it. Visitors may experience the object as meaningful, as entertaining, as a social device, as educational, as nostalgic, as research, as a personal connection, as identity, or as a representative of an event or person. Museum workers, too, could experience the museum object these ways, but they might also see it in the context of preservation, representation, evidence, a catalog entry, a part of a story, a design element, memory, or in other ways. Museum workers may think about the object in

Figure 3.5 Adaptation of Keene's (2002) concept of a system showing the specific feedback loops in the museum.

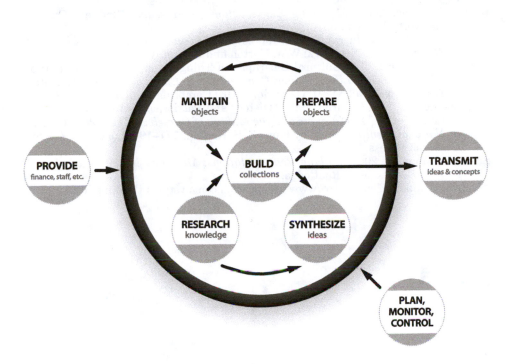

both the here and now as well as the past and the future. Both people and objects are a part of a network of activity, experience, and ideas. Networks are systems of interrelated and interconnecting units, a complicated and nonlinear set of channels that can inform and communicate across a multitude of linkages that are not always direct. In a museum, the network concept describes the flow of experiences and ideas through both staff and visitor relationships developed across, around, and through objects. In the networked museum model, the objects—all of the things in the museum—anchor the webs of information and people across all aspects of museum work, and each of these linkages represents a relationship. More details about these relationships are discussed in Chapter 6 in an exploration of the document-centered museum model.

References

Bell, Joshua A. 2012. "Museums as Relational Entities: The Politics and Poetics of Heritage." *Reviews in Anthropology* 41, no. 1: 70–92.

Capra, Fritjof. n.d. "The New Facts of Life." *EcoLiteracy*. http://www.ecoliteracy.org/essays/new-facts-life.

Cummins, Alissandra. 1994. "The Caribbeanization of the West Indies: The Museum's Role in the Development of National Identity." In *Museums and the Making of Ourselves: The Role of Objects in National Identity*, edited by Flora E.S. Kaplan, 192–220. London: Leicester University Press.

Humphrey, Philip S. 1976. "Course Notes." Lecture notes from the University of Kansas, Lawrence.

Humphrey, Philip S. 1991. "The Nature of University Natural History Museums." In *Natural History Museums: Directions for Growth*, edited by Paisley S. Cato and Clyde Jones, 5–11. Lubbock: Texas Tech University Press.

Keene, Suzanne. 2002. *Managing Conservation in Museums*. 2nd ed. Oxford: Butterworth-Heinemann.

Kerr, Michael E., and Murray Bowen. 1988. *Family Evaluation. An Approach Based on Bowen Theory*. New York: W.W. Norton and Company.

Kopytoff, Igor. 1986. "The Cultural Biography of Things: Commoditization as Process." In *The Social Life of Things: Commodities in Cultural Perspective*, edited by Arjun Appadurai, 64–91. Cambridge, UK: Cambridge University Press.

Morales-Moreno, Luis Gerardo. 1994. "History and Patriotism in the National Museum of Mexico." In *Museums and the Making of Ourselves: The Role of Objects in National Identity*, edited by Flora E. S. Kaplan, 171–191. London: Leicester University Press.

Simpson, Moira G. 2001. *Making Representations: Museums in the Post-Colonial Era*. Rev. ed. London: Routledge.

"Systems Thinking." n.d. http://www.pegasuscom.com/systems-thinking.html.

4

Dimensions of Museums

Functions of Museums

From the point of view of most visitors, what museums appear to do is collect objects and exhibit them. This perception is so deeply rooted in popular culture that a standard image of a museum in movies, books, and cartoons is a building full of dusty glass cases stuffed with objects and labels. How museums really function, however, is much more complex than this. Built into the definition of *museum*—"a system to build and permanently maintain an irreplaceable and meaningful physical resource and to use it to transmit ideas and concepts to the public" (Keene 2002)—are many functions that are either shrouded in mystery or not on the radar of many members of the public. This chapter explores how museums go about doing what they do—not just how objects are exhibited, but how collections are acquired, deaccessioned, and managed; how information about them is dispersed through public programming; the social functions that some museums perform; how collections are preserved; and the critical role of museum research.

In his book, *Introduction to Museology: The European Approach* (1998), Ivo Maroević identifies the critical functions of museums as preservation, research, and communication (see Figure 4.1). The way these three functions work together in the museum system gives museums their unique character as person-object-based institutions. In the following discussion the workings of the museum system are discussed in the context of these three functions.

Preservation

Throughout the history of museums, the preservation of objects in their collections—and the acknowledgment that they are worthy of such preservation because they hold unique information—has been a major concern. The survival of collections into the future is limited by the ways they are used and managed and by preservation technology—the materials and techniques used to care for objects. For example, many of the objects listed in catalogs or depicted in illustrations of Renaissance cabinets of curiosities have not survived the passage of time, due to the inadequacy of preservation

Figure 4.1   Three basic functions of the museum system. Adapted from Van Mensch (2004).

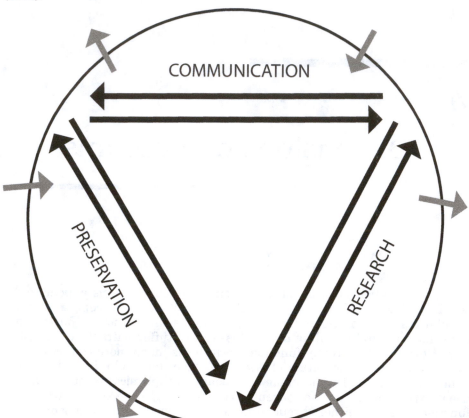

technology and collection management techniques. It has taken hundreds of years to develop a comprehensive understanding of why objects deteriorate and how to preserve them. Preservation in museums (protecting the objects in the collections from deterioration) is a delicate balance between the need to use the objects for exhibition, study, and research and the need to safeguard them in a stable storage environment for future generations. The dilemma for museums is how to make good use of their collections while carrying out aspects of their missions, because using the collections increases the risk of deterioration.

For hundreds of years the main focus of collections care was keeping the museum objects organized and properly labeled. Many processes of object deterioration progress so slowly that curators failed to notice the negative effects on the objects in their care (such as fading caused by exposure to sunlight). Advances in a variety of technical fields, including material sciences, conservation, and electronic data management, have contributed to improvements in the care of museum collections; as discussed in Chapter 7, these advances have affected the roles and duties of museum professionals. For example, collection managers and registrars incorporate the principles and practices of preventive conservation into their daily collections care activities, protecting the objects from the agents of deterioration and providing them with a stable storage environment. Beyond this daily work, there are also highly specialized conservators and conservation scientists who develop and help implement better collection care processes and procedures.

Restoration and Conservation

Part of the preservation function of museums is the practice of conservation, which grew out of the older practice of restoration. The profession of restoration—making objects that are old or damaged look new again—dates back to the Renaissance. For hundreds of years, restoration was shrouded in secrecy as restorers closely guarded the details of the procedures and materials they used, loathe to reveal their techniques to others. Unfortunately, many commonly used restoration practices and materials are detrimental to the long-term survival of the objects that are treated. Although a restorer might make an object look better, restoration rarely preserves the object's historical integrity or prolongs its useful life (the period of time during which information can be obtained from the object without loss of data). This situation changed in museums during the nineteenth century as a new profession arose that began to gradually displace the old, secret methods of the restorers: conservation. Two of the earliest workers to articulate the importance of preserving the historic and material integrity of museum objects were the English art expert John Ruskin, in his two most influential books, *The Seven Lamps of Architecture* and *The Stones of Venice*, and Eugène Viollet-le-Duc in France, in his *Dictionnaire raisonné de l'architecture française du XIe au XVe siècle*. The writings and ideas of Ruskin and Viollet-le-Duc inspired a generation of art restorers to deeply reconsider what they were doing and find ways to better preserve museum objects for the future. This led to the development of modern conservation; from the nineteenth century into the twentieth century, the principles and practices of conservation, grounded in science, gradually displaced those of restoration in museums. Although some of the practices and materials of conservation and restoration are similar, conservation takes a more scientific approach to objects than restoration by emphasizing thorough documentation of processes and the use of reversible materials and procedures. In other words, transparency replaced secrecy.

A restorer is concerned with the appearance of an object, whereas a conservator is concerned with how the object's history and materials affect its appearance. A good illustration of this is to consider the basic methodology applied to the conservation of a single object, which has been described as a series of eight steps by Barbara Appelbaum in *Conservation Treatment Methodology*:

- The object is carefully examined and described.

- The history of the object is researched and documented.

- A determination is made of what shall be considered the ideal state of the object (how the object should look after treatment).

- A realistic treatment goal is proposed.

- The methods and materials for treatment are selected and documented.

- The condition of the object prior to treatment is recorded in a detailed conservator's condition report.

- The treatment of the object is carried out by a trained conservator.

- The condition of the object after treatment is recorded in detail in another conservator's condition report.

Unlike restoration, conservators do not use secret methods or secret materials. Everything that is done to make an object look better or to stabilize it is carefully considered and documented, making the entire process transparent. Also unlike restoration, almost everything a conservator does must be reversible and identifiable so that the procedures can be undone if necessary in the future.

Conservation of a museum object is an expensive undertaking, as it requires an immense amount of time to be devoted to a single object, often uses costly materials and procedures, and is done by a person with specialized skills acquired through years of training. As a result, only the largest museums have on-staff conservators; most conservation work on individual objects in museums is contracted out to independent conservation professionals. Nevertheless, the development of the principles and practices of conservation have had a profound impact on how collections are managed. Beginning after about 1900, museums began to pay a lot more attention to how and why objects in their collections deteriorated. As a result of the concern for long-term collections care, the professions of registrar and collections manager arose in museums.

Preventive Conservation

Since the mid-1970s, collections care in museums has been dominated by the theory and practice of preventive conservation—the concept of taking measures to prolong the useful life of objects in collections—such as by providing a stable storage environment, controlling pests, and limiting the object's exposure to light. Preventive conservation was introduced in response to a growing awareness that many traditional collections care practices failed to address the deterioration of collections. In practice, preventive conservation emphasizes collection assessment, risk management, responses to the agents that cause deterioration of objects, and strategic planning. According to the theory of preventive conservation, the useful life of an object in a collection can be prolonged through four interrelated activities:

- Preventive care (avoiding deterioration)
- Treatment of damaged objects
- Research on ways to conserve objects
- Documentation of conservation activities

It is far more cost effective, and much better for the collections, to prevent their deterioration than to try to recover from deterioration. By understanding the factors that cause objects and specimens to deteriorate, collections care resources can be better applied to the long-term preservation of the objects.

A key aspect of preventive conservation is coping with the ten agents of deterioration of collection objects (developed at the Canadian Conservation Institute n.d.):

- *physical forces* (sudden impact, vibration, abrasion);
- *thieves and vandals*;

- *dissociation* (disordering that causes a separation of objects and information);
- *fire*;
- *water*;
- *collection pests*;
- *pollutants* in the form of gases or particles;
- *radiation* (ultraviolet, visible, and infrared);
- *incorrect temperatures*; and
- *incorrect relative humidity*.

Responses to these ten agents of deterioration include

- avoiding the agent;
- impeding or blocking the actions of the agent;
- detecting damage that occurs due to the agent;
- responding to deterioration caused by the agent, and
- recovering from damage after it has occurred in the collection.

Collection Management

Collection management refers to everything that is done to safeguard a musealized object (one added to the museum collection) from the ten agents of deterioration, prolong its useful life in the collection, and make the object and its associated information available to users. The management of an object begins with registration and continues throughout the life of the object in the museum's collection and beyond, because object records are maintained even after an object is no longer in the collection.

Registration and Collections Management

The overall process through which objects are musealized is called *registration*. Registration includes establishing the right of ownership for an object, forming a link between the object and its associated information, and adding it to the museum collection inventory. If the registration system is inadequate, it may cause a loss in value of a museum collection object (e.g., by allowing the object to be dissociated from its documentation or tracking numbers). Depending on the museum, registration may include any number of several separate processes, including acquisition, accession, cataloging, numbering, marking, and labeling.

Acquisition refers to the processes involved in obtaining objects for the collection (e.g., purchase, field collection, excavation, trade, donation). Once an object is accepted for inclusion in the museum collection, it is *accessioned* (the ownership of the object is legally transferred to the museum). As part of the accessioning process, the object is assigned an *accession number* that is used to track the object and any associated documentation. The accessioning process produces an *accession record*, which includes the documents that record information about the origin, history, and ownership of the object. In some museums, rather than using the accession number to track individual objects, the objects are instead assigned a *registration number* or *catalog*

Figure 4.2   Cataloged and numbered specimens, Earth and Mineral Sciences Museum & Art Gallery, Penn State University. Photograph by the authors.

number for tracking. In any case, all museum objects are assigned unique numbers that are used to identify them. The identifying number (accession, registration, or catalog number) is either marked directly on the object (Figure 4.2) or marked on a tag or label that is affixed to the object. The way that identifying numbers are marked or tags are attached should be reversible but secure.

Once accessioned and marked with an identifying number, the object is assigned a place in the *collection storage array* (the system used to keep the collection in order in storage, including the storage furniture and physical supports used to protect the object). Storage arrays vary greatly from one museum to another, due to differences in types of collection objects, available space and funds, and how the collection is used. Some general ordering systems that form the basis of collection storage arrays are described in Table 4.1. The system used in the collection storage array should be designed so that there is only one location in which each object is placed. This minimizes the misplacement and possible loss of objects.

Because museum objects spend most of their lives in storage, the collection management system must include a stable storage environment to help prolong the object's useful life. Note that exhibition is a form of storage and should also have appropriate environmental and security safeguards.

Registration includes periodic inventory of the contents of a collection and systems that track the objects when they are not in the storage array. Collection inventories vary from annual object-by-object examination in small collections to schedules that provide periodic checks of select parts of the collections in larger museums. The accession, registration, or catalog numbers are used to track objects that are removed from collection storage for use in exhibitions, programming, for research or study, or to be loaned to other institutions (see "Access to Objects and Object Information" below).

Because collections and museums change over time, objects may sometimes need to be *deaccessioned* from the collection. Deaccessioning is the

Table 4.1   Generalized Ordering Systems in Collection Storage Arrays

Type of Museum	Ordering System
Art	Artist's name Period Medium (material of composition) Genre
Natural history	Based on taxonomic ordering systems
Geosciences	Epochs Strata Chemical composition
History	Material (composition) Topical class (how object was used) Style Chenhall nomenclatural system (Bourcier and Rogers 2010)
Anthropology	Material (composition) Geographic origin Cultural association

opposite of accessioning; it is the permanent removal of an object from the collection. Although the practice of deaccessioning is as old as collections, due to its legal and ethical aspects, it remains a controversial practice. Some people think that museums should keep the objects in their collections in perpetuity, but in practice this is rarely possible because objects may deteriorate, become irrelevant due to changing institutional missions, or become too expensive to maintain. Because museums are accountable for the acquisition, conservation, management, and care of collection objects, deaccessioning is an important tool of collections management that allows the museum's resources to be used only for objects in the collections that help the museum fulfill its mission. Another area of controversy is how proceeds are used when a deaccesioned object is sold. The American Alliance of Museums takes the ethical position that all proceeds from deaccessioning should only be used for direct care of the collection, but some museum professionals disagree with this stance.

In a thoughtful essay, former museum administrator and legal expert Stephen E. Weil (1987) makes three important points regarding deaccessioning decisions:

- The retention of each and every object in a collection involves an ongoing expense for the museum (e.g., the storage, care, and management costs).

- Deaccessioning is sometimes used to generate funds that can be used to acquire other objects more critical to the museum's mission and collecting plan.

- Deaccessioning an object to another museum, particularly a peer institution, may better serve the museum community, the discipline, and the object itself.

Deaccessioning typically takes place when a museum exchanges an object with or gives one to another institution or when an object is determined to be no longer suitable to keep in the collection. Because there is always a cost involved with housing and caring for each object in the collection, deaccessioning helps museums use their collections care resources more wisely. Deaccessioning should be carefully considered and documented, and the object records should be maintained permanently by the museum, even after the deaccessioned object is no longer in the museum's possession.

Access to Objects and Object Information

For most of their history, access to collections and associated information was strictly controlled in museums, but it is now widely recognized that the public should have reasonable access to objects and information about them. This does not mean that everything has to be available at any time. Rather, reasonable access allows the museum to establish restrictions based on the fragility of objects, on the sensitivity of collection information, or in consideration of cultural practices and beliefs associated with certain objects. For example, the Makah Cultural and Research Center in Neah Bay, Washington, has a collection of recordings as part of its oral history program held in the tribal archives. However, the recordings are only made available for use with the permission of Makah elders, because some tribal knowledge is restricted and cannot be shared with nontribal members. In another case, Hopi elders cautioned the staff at the Field Museum in Chicago that, based on their tribal belief system, it was inappropriate for pregnant women, even those who were not Native Americans, to work with Hopi kachinas in the collection. In other museums, an ongoing research project by a scholar may preempt other researchers from using part of the collection or collection records for a specified time period.

One important way that museum collections are made available is through loans of objects to peer institutions for exhibition or study. The borrowing and loaning of collection objects is an important museum practice. A *loan* is a temporary custody arrangement without a change of ownership; thus loans are always of limited duration. Because a loan is a temporary transfer of an object, a loan agreement should always include a termination date. Long-term loans and open-ended loans (those that do not have an end date or renewal date) were once fairly common in museums but are now recognized as contrary to best practices. The term *permanent loan* was once common, but it is an oxymoron and should no longer be used. The loan of an object from a museum collection is a legal contract, and like all contracts, the terms of the arrangement should be included in the loan documentation.

Legally, there are three broad types of loans, each with different responsibilities for the care of the objects involved, based on which party to the contract receives the most benefit from the loan. When a loan is for the primary benefit of the lender, it is the lender who bears most of the responsibility (e.g., a museum undergoing renovation might arrange for another institution to borrow part of its collection to make room for the renovation work to be done). The most common type of loan is one that is for the primary benefit of the borrower, which means the borrowing institution bears primary responsibility for the care of the objects. In some cases, the loan may be for the mutual benefit of both parties, in which case the institutions share responsibility equally.

Ultimately, the museum staff has the duty to care for its collections in ways that achieve a balance between conservation and use. In all cases, increased handling and disruption of the stable storage environment ultimately shorten the useful life of objects. Each time an object is removed from storage, it is placed at greater risk of deterioration or damage. Some objects are simply too fragile to be loaned (or, in rare cases, even to be exhibited); other objects can only be exhibited for limited amounts of time because they are so susceptible to damage and the agents of deterioration. Museum staff must make decisions about physical access on a case-by-case basis, weighing the needs of the users with the care of the object, to determine what can and cannot be done. Museums can make their collections more accessible while still protecting them by making images of the objects and their associated information available online, as virtual exhibits, in user-accessible databases, and by other means. Some museums make detailed, digitized images of objects available both online and via computer stations in the exhibit galleries. More and more museums today are putting their collection databases online for users to access.

Electronic Data Management

Few standards for registration or collections management systems existed prior to the introduction of electronic database systems beginning in the late 1970s and early 1980s. Although almost all museums had systems for the registration and tracking of their collection objects and associated information, these systems varied widely, sometimes even between departments within the same museum. Records were either handwritten or typed on file cards, in bound ledger books, or on sheets of paper in file folders or notebooks.

Museums began using computers only after libraries demonstrated how effective they could be in managing large amounts of information, but the lack of standardized registration procedures and robust nomenclatural systems in museums has hindered progress. Nevertheless, computerization has made it possible for museums to make much more information available to museum users, and thanks to digitization and virtual exhibits, has allowed museums to provide electronic access to more of their collections.

A computerized collection database has two basic functions. First, it makes access to the collection records rapid and efficient, allows new ways of accessing data, and reduces transcription errors. Second, a good database is a valuable collection management tool that can be used for collection inventories, loan records, tracking of objects on exhibit or undergoing treatment, condition reporting, tracking the history of the use of the object, re-sorting of information for new uses, integrated pest management (tracking outbreaks and treatments, monitoring for pest activity), planning for collection moves or rehousing, and other uses.

Research

Without museological research, museums would be little more than warehouses full of objects. Nevertheless, research is the function of museums that is least understood and most often overlooked or ignored. Museum research begins with the objects in the collection, but extends well beyond them to information about the objects and the connective web of interrelations surrounding those objects. Museological research includes investigations of object provenance (history of ownership), significance, and historical and cultural associations but may also include studies on the form or materials of objects, their manufacture, their use, or their cultural or scientific value. Generally, the purpose of research in a museum relates to the collection or museum itself, the creation of an exhibition, or scholarly inquiry (both museological and discipline content specific). The sort of research done in a particular museum depends mainly on the characteristics of the collection, the information available about it, and the interests of the researcher.

Some authors have argued that during the latter part of the twentieth century, research shifted from museums to universities, but this is only partially true. A substantial amount of research is still being produced in museums, but it is often overshadowed by the amount of research now emanating from universities. As Conn (1998) pointed out, early in the last century American universities were little more than finishing schools, while most of the original research was done in museums. During the second half of the twentieth century universities became more research oriented, and the amount of research they now produce is much greater than that coming from museums, even though research remains an important function in many museums. One reason that museum research is often overlooked is that much of the work done using museum collections is done by researchers from universities and other institutions who are not museum staff members.

Most current museum research consists of object-based investigations. For example, the majority of research in natural history museums is directly based on the use of collections, such as the identification of new species of plants and animals and their evolutionary relationships, which requires analysis of large numbers of specimens. In anthropology museums, most object-based research comes from the study of material culture, which also requires comprehensive collections. Larger art museums and most university art museums produce significant research based on the objects in their collections, particularly the scholarship that goes into many exhibition catalogs. On the other hand, most historians, with some notable exceptions, do not make extensive use of objects in their research.

In almost all museums, the interpretation of collections through exhibitions, public programming, and so forth requires extensive research. In addition to the direct use of objects in this work, most of the research that underlies conservation of individual objects (often referred to as bench conservation) and preventive conservation is based on the use of museum collections. Museum collections have high research value due to several factors, including the documented history of individual objects (provenance), the number and variety of objects available to researchers, the order and arrangement of objects in the collection storage array, the deep history of most museum collections (a variety of related objects acquired over many decades), and the fact that museum collections are generally and comparatively well cared for.

Communication

Communication takes many forms, from the personal to the organizational. In museums, communication is constant, as it is the business of museums to communicate about their contents to their various audiences. The definition of museum used in this book states that one of the main jobs of the museum is to "transmit ideas and concepts to the public." In the past, this transmission was largely unidirectional, with curators deciding what would be exhibited by determining or selecting what information visitors would see. While that still occurs, there is now a loop back from the visitors, making communication in museums a two-way street. Communication is part of a cycle of information transfer in museums. From an information perspective, museums are concerned with the

- generation,
- perpetuation,
- organization, and
- dissemination of information.

The *generation of information* results from research and study of collections in the museum or from their context in the museum. Information is generated primarily from the objects in the collections, but also from conservation activities, collections care and management activities, exhibition of the collections, the creation of programs, research based on the collections, and so forth.

Perpetuation of information refers to the preservation and conservation of collections and the collection documentation. This includes both the original information connected with the objects, as well as information and knowledge generated by use and interpretation of the collections.

The *organization of information* involves establishing relationships between discrete elements of information, linking data to objects in the collection, and the use of classification or organizational schemes to make museum information available. In the past, the quantity of information to be managed and the length of time it took to organize it limited what was available to users. One of the great benefits of electronic data management is that museums can now organize much more information in many more categories than in the past, thus better fulfilling museum missions and better serving the public.

Dissemination of information requires creating and maintaining open channels to information. This includes access to records and the collection objects themselves, exhibitions, educational programming, and publication (to publish means to make public and thus includes print, film, electronic, and other means).

In museums, communication is involved in nearly everything the museum does. A number of aspects of communication are highlighted below that are central to museum functioning, including communication with the public, communication through interpretation, sociocultural communication, and personal communication, particularly in the forms of inspiration and meaning-making. These are not the only forms of communication in museums, but they are the most prevalent and help in elucidating the function of communication in museums.

Communication with the Public

In the Hellenistic period, the forerunners of modern museums were places where private collections were used by an elite selection of teachers to educate their chosen students. During the Renaissance, museums—in the form of cabinets of curiosities—served a broader audience, made up of the rich and powerful, scholars, and a few artists. From early modern times onward, museums have increasingly been used to educate the general public as well as other museum users. In some instances, museums have become agents of interpretation and social change. More recently, trends in exhibition strategies and the advance of visitor studies have enabled museums to become more user-centered, thereby increasing and enhancing communication with museum audiences.

Communication through Interpretation

Communication in museums is based partly on the interpretation of musealized objects to the museum's audiences. Interpretation refers to a communication process that is designed to reveal relationships and meanings through the use of objects, illustrative media, and narratives. It is not simply communicating factual information, but rather involves strategy, translation, principles, and techniques. Interpretation can be powerful, if done well, and draws out emotion and inspiration as well as intellect. In *Museums in Motion* (2008), Edward Alexander and Mary Alexander describe the basic elements of modern museum interpretation:

- Interpretation has an educational purpose (to reveal meaning, to impart understanding).
- Interpretation is based on objects.
- Interpretation is supported by object research, audience research, and program analysis.
- Interpretation uses sensory perception along with words and verbalization.
- Interpretation is part of informal learning.

Sociocultural Communication

Museums have evolved in many ways in response to societal pressures and demands. A recent example is that few museums now exhibit the human remains of Native Americans the same way they were exhibited as recently as twenty years ago. Responding to societal pressures can be problematic for museums, because the interpretation of certain objects often produces a clash of cultures. For instance, one culture wants its objects and knowledge respected and treated in a certain way, while another culture finds altruistic reasons that the same objects and knowledge should be made available to the general public. One critic (Tiffany Jenkins n.d.) has argued that restrictions on some objects as a result of museums' sensitivity to religious and cultural ideals have endangered the concept of public access to museum collections. Some cases make this point:

- At the Hancock Museum in Newcastle, UK, female staff members were told that they are not allowed to look at male *churinga* totems in the collection that come from the Arrernte of Australia;
- At the Victoria and Albert Museum in London, some collections of Christian artifacts have been arranged separately from collections of Jewish artifacts, based on input from religious advisors.

These examples demonstrate how difficult such situations can be to negotiate. On the one hand, museums want to be respectful of cultural traditions, but on the other, museums should be open to all members of the public to allow them to benefit from the collections. There is no easy, one-size-fits-all solution for these dilemmas; each must be resolved carefully, taking into consideration all of the information and opinions available. Members of the invested communities may be recruited to provide input and are sometimes organized as a standing community board. For example, leaders from the associated Native American communities might be invited to meet with museum staff and anthropologists to discuss whether or not certain objects should be exhibited at all, and if so, how they should be interpreted and displayed. Although there is a growing literature on how such decisions have been made in museums that can provide some guidance (e.g., Dubin 1999; Mihesuah 2000; Sherman 2008; Simpson 2001; Sleeper-Smith 2009), finding the best solution is never easy.

REALITY CHECK

Cultural Value of Objects

Knowledge and cultural values are socially constructed. Some cultural values are glaringly obvious, but others may be so subtle they are easily overlooked. For example, the Liberty Bell is an object that today is seen as emblematic of the American Revolution. The Liberty Bell draws thousands of visitors each year, even though it is now housed in an entirely different context than the one that is the basis of its iconic status. In fact, the Liberty Bell is an example of an object that only became iconic due to later cultural gloss applied to it. The bell, which cracked while being rung not long after it arrived in the colonies from London, is presumed to have been one of those rung in Philadelphia on July 8, 1776, when the Declaration of Independence was first read in public, but there is no evidence to support this claim. The bell didn't acquire its emblematic status until nearly seventy-five years after the American Revolution, when it was featured in an 1847 short story that was widely read. The bell was originally hung in the Pennsylvania State House, which later became Independence Hall; in 1976 it was moved to the nearby Liberty Bell Center, where visitors now line up for hours to see it. Oddly enough, far more people stand in line to see the Liberty Bell, now isolated in a glass room, than line up to tour Independence Hall, which by any standard is a site of major significance to the history of the United States. That the iconic status of the Liberty Bell is so much greater than the iconic status of Independence Hall can only be understood in the context of how cultural values are shaped, and it is these cultural values that give importance to many museum objects.

Although all objects have some material value (also called market value), in museums objects may be more valued for their cultural affiliations. Material value is also a social construct, even though it rests more on the physicality of the object than its cultural association. For example, consider silver and gold, both of which have long had high material value, particularly in European cultures. At the time the Spanish arrived in the Americas, the gold and silver that the Spanish were seeking were not considered by the Incas to be as valuable as wool from the vicuña, a small relative of the llama that lives at high altitude in the Andes. The Incas used gold and silver for public decoration and adornment, but only members of the highest levels of the Inca royalty were allowed to wear garments woven from vicuña wool. The Incas assigned a high cultural value to gold and silver because both were considered divine metals, but their belief system did not recognize the same intrinsic material value that the Spanish attached to them. These differences made it possible for the captured Inca ruler, Atahualpa, to fill a room that measured 22 by 17 feet to a height of 8 feet—once with gold and twice with silver—in just two months in an attempt to gain his freedom from the Spanish. Among the ironies of the Spanish lust for riches are that the intricate, handmade gold and silver objects that were melted down for easy shipment back to Spain would be worth far more today had they not been melted into ingots, and that vicuña wool is still the most expensive natural fiber in the world.

Personal Communication: Inspiration and Meaning-Making

As the purposes and roles of museums in communities continue to be refined, their staff members strive to enable stronger connections for visitors in their learning and meaning-making. In doing so, it is vital that they pay close attention to their visitors' personal connections to objects and ideas within the museum. Museum staff are coming to understand that the content and meaning of their collections are different for every visitor who comes to see them. Making meaning is a critical aspect of interactions with and interpretation of museum objects, exhibits, and programs. The way collections are managed, interpreted, and presented can affect the way people interact with the objects to make meaning (e.g., through object accessibility and ease of locating associated information).

Meaning-making in the museum involves learning, which has been defined as a dynamic process involving the construction of new ideas and understandings through interaction with objects and their cultural associations (Tishman 2007). In museums, visitors derive meaning from objects in three ways: from the documentation that supports the objects; from the interpretation of objects; and from their interrelationships with people and things around them, which includes the visitors themselves (Maroević 1998). The successful functioning of museums depends on the act of intentionally striving to attain rich visitor experience. Information and objects may have value independently, but when there is a connection between the object and its associated information, and the characteristics of the individual visitors, the quality and significance of both are increased. When people are able to make personal connections with the objects, it can produce powerful experiences for them, creating lasting memories and increasing the value the public places on museums (Wood and Latham 2013).

References

Alexander, Edward Porter, and Mary Alexander. 2008. *Museums in Motion: An Introduction to the History and Functions of Museums*. Lanham, MD: Altamira Press.

Appelbaum, Barbara. 2010. *Conservation Treatment Methodology*. New York: CreateSpace.

Bourcier, Paul, and Ruby Rogers. 2010. *Nomenclature 3.0 for Museum Cataloging: Third Edition of Robert G. Chenhall's System for Classifying Man-Made Objects*. Lanham, MD: Altamira Press.

Buck, Rebecca A., and Jean Allman Gilmore. 2010. *MRM5: Museum Registration Methods*. 5th ed. Washington, DC: American Association of Museums Press.

Canadian Conservation Institute. n.d. "Ten Agents of Deterioration." http://www .cci-icc.gc.ca/caringfor-prendresoindes/articles/10agents/index-eng.aspx.

Conn, Steven. 1998. *Museums and American Intellectual Life, 1876–1926*. Chicago: University of Chicago Press.

Cummins, Alissandra. 1994. "The Caribbeanization of the West Indies: The Museum's Role in the Development of National Identity." In *Museums and the Making of Ourselves: The Role of Objects in National Identity*, edited by Flora E. S. Kaplan, 192–220. London: Leicester University Press.

Dierking, Lynn D. 2002. "The Role of Context in Children's Learning from Objects and Experience." In *Perspectives on Object-Centered Learning in Museums*, edited by Scott G. Paris, 3–16. Mahwah, NJ: Lawrence Erlbaum Associates.

Dubin, S. C. 1999. *Displays of Power: Controversy in the American Museum from the Enola Gay to Sensation*. New York: New York University Press.

Falk, John H. 2002. Foreword to *The Role of Context in Children's Learning from Objects and Experience: Perspectives on Object-Centered Learning in Museums*, edited by Scott G. Paris, ix–xiii. Mahwah, NJ: Lawrence Erlbaum Associates.

Falk, John Howard, and Lynn Diane Dierking. 2000. *Learning from Museums: Visitor Experiences and the Making of Meaning*. Walnut Creek, CA: Altamira Press.

Hein, George E. 1998. *Learning in the Museum*. New York: Routledge.

Jenkins, Tiffany. n.d. "The Censoring of Our Museums." https://www.newstatesman.com/node/151066.

Keene, Suzanne. 2002. *Managing Conservation in Museums*. 2nd ed. Oxford: Butterworth-Heinemann.

Maroević, Ivo. 1998. *Introduction to Museology: The European Approach*. Munich: C. Müller-Straten.

Mihesuah, Devon Abbott, ed. 2000. *Repatriation Reader: Who Owns American Indian Remains?* Lincoln: University of Nebraska Press.

Morales-Moreno, Luis Gerardo. 1994. "History and Patriotism in the National Museum of Mexico." In *Museums and the Making of Ourselves: The Role of Objects in National Identity*, edited by Flora E. S. Kaplan, 171–191. London: Leicester University Press.

Muñoz Viñas, Salvador. 2005. *Contemporary Theory of Conservation*. Amsterdam: Elsevier.

Paris, Scott G. 2002. "Children Learning with Objects in Informal Learning Environments." In *Perspectives on Object-Centered Learning in Museums*, edited by Scott G. Paris, 37–54. Mahwah, NJ: Lawrence Erlbaum Associates.

Ruskin, John. 1889. *The Seven Lamps of Architecture*. 6th ed. Sunnyside, Orpington, UK: G. Allen.

Ruskin, John. 1911. *The Stones of Venice*. Boston: Estes and Lauriat.

Sherman, D. J., ed. 2008. *Museums and Difference*. Bloomington: Indiana University Press.

Simpson, Moira G. 2001. *Making Representations: Museums in the Post-colonial Era*. Rev. ed. London: Routledge.

Sleeper-Smith, Susan, ed. 2009. *Contesting Knowledge: Museums and Indigenous Perspectives*. Lincoln: University of Nebraska Press.

Tilden, F. 1957. *Interpreting Our Heritage: Principles and Practices for Visitor Services in Parks, Museums, and Historic Places*. Chapel Hill: University of North Carolina Press.

Tishman, Shari, et al. 2007. *Study Center Learning: An Investigation of the Educational Power and Potential of the Harvard University Art Museums Study Centers*. Cambridge, MA: Harvard University Art Museums.

Van Mensch, Peter. 2004. "Museology and Management: Enemies or Friends? Current Tendencies in Theoretical Museology and Museum Management in Europe." In *Museum Management in the 21st Century*, edited by E. Mizushima, 3–19. Tokyo: Museum Management Academy.

Viollet-le-Duc, E.-E. 1856. *Dictionnaire raisonné de l'architecture française du XIe au XVIe siècle*. Paris: B. Bance.

Weil, Stephen. 1987. "Deaccession Practices in American Museums." *Museum News* 65, no. 3: 44–49.

Wood, E., and Kiersten F. Latham. 2009. "Object Knowledge: Researching Objects in the Museum Experience." *Reconstruction* 9, no. 1.

Wood, Elizabeth, and Kiersten F. Latham. 2013. *The Objects of Experience: Transforming Visitor-Object Encounters in Museums*. Walnut Creek, CA: Left Coast Press.

Section Three
What

5

Species of Museums:
A Museological Bestiary

The Many Varieties of Museums

In the exploration of museums as systems, it was noted that the similarities among museums are more significant than their differences In this chapter, various kinds of museums, or *species of museums,* are considered. In examining some traditional categories of museums, as well as a few not-so-traditional categories, it is important to keep in mind that from the systems perspective, museums and other museal institutions have their own structures, processes, and conceptual bases that include all kinds of museums, regardless of the content of their collections. Although the content of the museum (what is in the collection) may appear to be more significant than the museological (conceptual) and the museographical (practical) aspects of museum work, it really isn't. At the end of the day, all museum collections must be cared for and made accessible for use, no matter what sorts of things they contain. The content of collections and how the objects are used is obviously important, but there is much more to museum work than knowing a subject discipline. For example, a person could be an expert on tropical frogs or medieval Dutch art, but that alone would not be sufficient qualification to manage a collection of tropical frogs or medieval Dutch art. It is knowing the museological and museographical aspects of collections work that makes someone a successful museum collections professional.

Why consider species of museums at all? There are often good reasons for grouping museums by categories. For example, it can help those working in museums to identify peer institutions for purposes of seeking advice or potential new homes for collection objects; categories of museums are often used by funding agencies to make sure that they allocate their resources appropriately; the distinctions are useful for the public in deciding which museums they would like to visit; and taxonomies of museums may identify gaps in the systems of protection for natural and cultural heritage.

When most people think about museums, they usually have in mind one of the big three categories: art, history, and natural history. However, as discussed in Chapter 2, museums did not start out as specialized institutions; they started out as collections of objects. As collections grew larger and larger during the Renaissance, the word *museum* was used to describe them, no matter what sorts of objects they contained. It was much later in museum history that these object-based, collecting institutions came to be identified by categories such as *art* museums or *science* museums.

The most profound change, however, that has come to modern museums since their origin has been specialization, which occurred as museum collections expanded in size and scope, making it difficult for a single institution to collect broadly and maintain the expertise necessary to interpret a vast array of objects. Over the last century the concepts of theme and mission have also played a role in the specialization of museums, as museums defined their roles and purposes more clearly, and many small museums have been created that are intentionally narrowly focused in their missions.

There are still big, all-encompassing museums that seem to collect everything; these institutions are sometimes called universal, or general, museums. A perfect example of a universal museum is the venerable British Museum, founded in London in 1753 to show off its already vast collections of anthropological artifacts, art, history, and science, as well as its library. As the British Museum has grown, some of its collections have been split off into other institutions, such as The Natural History Museum and the British Library. By contrast, another universal museum, the Royal Ontario Museum in Toronto, Canada, has grown extensively since its founding in 1912 but has remained a single institution and is widely recognized as one of the world's premier museums. Most people think of the Smithsonian Institution as a single universal museum, but it started as a natural science museum and grew into a sprawling complex of nineteen museums, a zoo, and nine research centers.

Museums may also be categorized by size, theme, budget, collection content, mission, audience, and many more characteristics. None of these categorization schemes is definitive, and in fact, most of the categorical distinctions in any scheme are pretty fuzzy (e.g., just how does one distinguish among small, medium, and large museums?), but many of them are useful for purposes of comparison.

Certainly there is a bewildering variety of museums in the world. No precise count of the number of museums in the United States is available, partly because of the problem of defining what museums are (as discussed in Chapter 1). Estimates range from around 17,500 museums, according to the American Alliance of Museums (n.d.), to around 30,000, according to Heritage Preservation; the latter estimate includes archives, libraries, scientific research collections, and archaeological repositories. From a survey conducted by Heritage Preservation (2005), estimates of the total number of objects in collections in U.S. museums are also broad, ranging up to 4.8 billion objects. This is an impressive number, particularly in light of the fact that 75 percent of museums in the United States were founded after 1950. In any case, U.S. museums host around 2.5 billion visitors each year, bring in about $9 billion, and employ nearly 80,000 workers.

According to the most recently available data for the United States (see Table 5.1), history museums and historic sites make up 55.3 percent of museums; another 14.8 percent are art museums; and all other museums combined make up the remaining 29.9 percent.

In the United States, 60 percent of museums are private and 40 percent are government institutions. Most government-owned museums are at the state and local levels; only 7 percent of U.S. museums are part of the federal government. Most museums are modest in size: a mere 8 percent have

Table 5.1   U.S. Museums by Type

Type of Museum	Percentage of U.S. Museums
History	29.8
Historic sites	25.5
Art	14.8
General (more than one type of collection)	8.6
Specialized	5.7
Botanical gardens and arboretums	3.8
Nature centers	3.6
Natural history and anthropology	3.0
Science centers	2.2
Zoological parks	1.6
Children's museums	0.8
Planetariums	0.5
Aquariums	0.2

Based on data from the Institute of Museum and Library Services (n.d.).

annual budgets of more than $1 million, 57 percent have budgets of $100,000 or less, and 38 percent have budgets under $50,000. Where do these budget dollars come from? The sources of support for U.S. museums are also quite varied, with 36.5 percent of support coming from donors, 27.6 percent coming from earned income (mostly entrance fees and gift shop sales), 24.4 percent from government sources (local, state, and federal combined), and 11.5 percent from investments (Bell 2012).

Whatever the actual number of museums is in the United States, it includes art museums, national museums, historic houses, music museums, mustard museums, and of course zoos, aquariums, and botanical gardens. Other types include children's museums, military museums, wax museums, halls of fame, battlefield museums, nature centers, planetariums, and presidential libraries. Adding to the list are technology centers, corporate museums, folk art museums, medical museums, science centers, and transportation museums, not to mention those new museums that exist only in cyberspace. In this chapter museums are sorted and resorted into several categories to get a better picture of their variety and basic structure.

The Traditional Categories: Discipline-Based Museums

Museums that are based on a particular area of study—subject-discipline-based museums, or more simply discipline-based museums—are what most people have in mind when they think about museums. The big three are art, history, and natural history, but these categories are very broad. For example, art museums include everything from large, comprehensive institutions that collect art from almost any time period or geographic location, to museums devoted to the art of a specific region, to an individual artist or even a particular period in the life of an individual artist. The same holds true for the other two traditional discipline-based museum types. The more traditional and better-known types of museums (art, history, and natural history and anthropology museums) are considered in greater detail below.

Art Museums

As noted above, museums of art range from general institutions, such as the Metropolitan Museum of Art in New York City, to those devoted to art produced by a particular artist, such as the Salvador Dali Museum in Figueres, Spain, to art from a specific geographic area, such as the New England Regional Art Museum in Armidale, Australia. The category of art museums includes museums that primarily collect fine art, craft and applied art, and folk art. Art museums are based on aesthetic philosophy and critical reflections on the nature and appreciation of art and its place in culture. What constitutes art, and which artworks should be included in museum collections, are decisions made by curators who have developed their expertise as scholars and connoisseurs. Most of the objects collected by art museums are intended for exhibition. Historically, art museums have not appealed to the broad general public, but rather to a well-educated and generally well-to-do subset of the public. However, most art museums now try to attract a broader audience.

In the United States, the development of art museums has been influenced by their educational emphasis, though education has never been as strong a force in art museums as the aesthetics of collection building. Evidence of the influence of aesthetics in art museums is revealed through the amount of interpretation associated with objects on display. Standing in the exhibition space of a traditional art museum, one of the most distinctive features is the amount of text on the labels. Art museums usually provide very little text, and less frequently interpretive text. In most other kinds of museums, objects have labels that interpret the object; art museum labels may simply identify the object. It is notable that many art museums are now breaking out of this routine by providing richer labels and more interpretation (e.g., the Detroit Institute of Arts and the Art Institute of Chicago). Other features of traditional art museums are that the objects collected are usually unique, one-of-a-kind, original creations, and their collections tend to be relatively small compared to staff size.

History Museums

History museums are usually focused on a geographic region (e.g., the Kansas Museum of History) or a specific time or event (e.g., the National Civil War Museum). Together, history museums and historic sites are the largest category of museum in the United States. Many of these museums are small, community enterprises, frequently with all-volunteer staffs, and they often serve as important centers of community life and community pride. Included in these smaller museums are many historic houses that are considered significant by the local community.

History museum collections tend to be larger relative to staff size than those of art museums. Objects collected by history museums are usually intended to document important persons, places, or events, or to be representative substitutes for such objects with direct historic connections. Collections in history museums, like those in art museums, are usually based on objects that are considered unique and important rather than common and typical, although recent trends in history collecting have been directed toward more comprehensive sampling of all aspects of society to provide a broader, more comprehensive reflection of culture. History museum collections, in general, are used far more extensively for exhibition and documentation than for research. Most historians are not object-oriented and do not work directly with objects. As a result, history museums are often focused much less on the object and more on the associated documentation and its information.

Natural History and Anthropology Museums

This category of a traditional, discipline-based museum includes natural history and anthropology museums with collections of well-documented objects and specimens collected primarily for research or scholarly use. Science centers, planetariums, discovery spaces, and similar institutions that teach scientific principles but do not have research collections are excluded from this category and are discussed below. Natural history and anthropology museums started as collections of oddities, rarities, and marvels, but beginning in the seventeenth century they evolved into centers of scientific inquiry. Natural history and anthropology collecting is based on scientific curiosity rather than connoisseurship or the historical associations of objects—specimens are generally selected for inclusion in collections because they are typical or representative, not because they are unique. Objects in natural history and anthropology museums are collected on a systematic basis, with an attempt to build representational collections that can be used to understand the natural world and human cultures. These collections tend to be very large relative to staff size, because scientific studies require a series of similar specimens or objects. Although many of these museums are associated with universities, there are also a number of significant independent institutions such as the Field Museum in Chicago, the American Museum of Natural History in New York, and the Natural History Museum in London.

Other Kinds of Museums

Museums are diverse and therefore too difficult to classify into a discrete array of types. However, in the next section a few more broad categories are briefly presented, including museums that are part of colleges and universities, living history museums, medical museums, specialized museums, science centers, community museums, and others.

University Museums

Museums associated with colleges and universities used to be much more common than they are now. Nevertheless, many such museums, though small, provide excellent training resources for students. Research on learning has demonstrated the importance of informal learning (that which takes place outside of a traditional classroom) at all stages of life; much—and perhaps most—of what students learn in college is learned in the campus environment, not in class, which underscores the importance of university museums.

Some university museum collections have a little bit of everything in accordance with their teaching missions (often called postage stamp style collections), while others have extensive research collections. Some relatively modest university museums have specialized collections that are recognized as world-class resources. For example, the Wilcox Classical Museum at the University of Kansas, founded in 1886, has nearly 700 objects, including rare plaster casts of Greek and Roman sculpture. Many collections of natural history specimens or anthropological objects are used purely as teaching or research collections and housed within their respective academic departments or in research facilities; because these collections are not open to the general public, they may not be considered museums. An example of a significant university museum that does not have public exhibits is the Museum of Vertebrate Zoology at the University of California Berkeley. The museum's 640,000 specimens are an important research resource for scientists worldwide, but due to the lack of exhibits, the museum does not meet the American Alliance of Museums standards for accreditation.

Living History and Agricultural Museums

Living history museums are those in which interpretive staff role-play historic people of a certain time or place, usually in the context of a house, farm, or plantation. These museums usually make use of at least some historic buildings, often moved from their original locations, and they have historically accurate costumed staff members who interact with museum visitors. The degree and type of engagement with the audience varies, from staff members who step out of character to talk to visitors about what they are doing to those who never break character in front of guests. Examples are Greenfield Village at The Henry Ford in Dearborn, Michigan, Conner Prairie Interactive History Park in Fishers, Indiana, and the Ukrainian Cultural Heritage Village in Alberta, Canada.

Medical Museums

Medical museums and anatomical museums (Figure 5.1) were once associated with almost every medical school in the Americas and Europe (and other places as well) to provide a place where medical students could examine specimens firsthand. Changes in the way medicine is taught, and improvements in the quality of illustrations available in medical textbooks, have diminished their importance to medical education. However, medical museums are still very popular with the public, and many now play important roles in community health education.

Medical and anatomical museums often have ghoulish reputations, whether deserved or not, such as the Siriraj Medical Museum in Bangkok. Although most of the guidebooks to Bangkok mention only that the body of the child murderer and cannibal Si Ouey Sae Urng is on exhibit, in truth the museum is used extensively by medical students from Siriraj Hospital, and its exhibits teach visitors much about health and medicine in Thailand. Similarly, the Mütter Museum at the College of Physicians in Philadelphia takes advantage of its reputation for shock value to attract visitors who, once inside, learn a lot about what makes us all human as well as the history of medicine in the United States.

REALITY CHECK

Shock Value and Value Shock

I have worked as a consultant at the Mütter Museum in Philadelphia, helping to rehouse many of its fluid preserved specimens. On several occasions I was at work in the public galleries when school groups came into the museum. Each time, I could hear the loud voices and false bravado of the kids as they came into the gallery, hoping to be grossed out and disgusted. Inevitably, each group would become quiet and somber, then fascinated as they gazed at the specimens and read the labels. I don't think I have ever seen more visitors reading labels than in the Mütter galleries. When time ran out and they had to leave, most of them talked about coming back for another visit. (JES)

Figure 5.1 Percy Skuy Gallery, Dittrick Museum of Medical History, Case Western Reserve University. Photo courtesy of Dittrick Museum.

Specialized Museums

There is a bewildering array of seemingly odd little museums often based on a theme or a genre of object, such as the European Asparagus Museum in Schrobenhausen, Germany, or the Martin and Osa Johnson Safari Museum in Chanute, Kansas. These places function as museum systems built around a meaningful physical resource (objects) with the purpose of transmitting ideas to a public. Most of these institutions are private museums, but they are museums nonetheless. In the United States, these small, specialized museums vary from the tiny (Figure 5.2) and ephemeral (sadly enough, the former Museum of Menstruation is now closed) to museums with established audiences and staying power, such as the Historic Voodoo Museum in New Orleans or the Havre de Grace Decoy Museum in Havre de Grace, Maryland. Some are based on humor, though they may also offer a serious critique of culture, such as the Museum of Bad Art in Dedham Square, Massachusetts, or the American International Rattlesnake Museum in Albuquerque, New Mexico. Some are intentionally established as commercial tourist destinations, such as the Museum of Death in San Diego, California, and the International Spy Museum in Washington, D.C.

One of the more fascinating of these specialized museums is the Museum of Jurassic Technology in Culver City, California, which may also be considered a long-term and dynamic art installation, produced by artist David Wilson. What sets the Museum of Jurassic Technology apart is the way it forces the visitor to undertake a critical assessment of what museums mean (it was also the subject of a delightful book by Lawrence Weschler, *Mr. Wilson's Cabinet of Wonder*).

Figure 5.2　The Traveler's Club International Restaurant and Tuba Museum, East Lansing, Michigan. Photo by authors.

Sometimes these specialized museums have collections significant enough that they are acquired by larger institutions. For example, the Museum of Questionable Medical Devices in Minneapolis is now part of the Science Museum of Minnesota. Even though they may be quirky or unusual, these enterprises function as museums and serve the same purposes as larger, more traditional institutions.

REALITY CHECK

Lessons in Obscurity

I once visited the Gallery of Wood Art in St. Paul, Minnesota, run by the American Association of Wood Turners, and commented to the person at the entrance desk that this had to be one of the most specialized associations around. "Oh, no," I was told. "We have 14,000 members! There is a meeting in town right now of a much smaller and stranger organization, the Society for the Preservation of Natural History Collections [SPNHC], which has less than 1,000 members." The reason I was in St. Paul was to attend the SPNHC annual conference. (JES)

Science Centers, Discovery Spaces, Planetariums, and Similar Institutions

Science centers and discovery spaces are designed primarily to teach people about science and technology and often focus on children and families as their primary audiences. These museums usually contain mostly interactive exhibits, and very few have permanent collections (or at least not very large collections). The number of institutions in this category has grown dramatically over the last three decades with the recognition of the importance of informal learning. Examples of science centers and discovery spaces are The Exploratorium (in San Francisco, California), the Please Touch Museum and the Franklin Institute (both in Philadelphia, Pennsylvania), and the Museum of Science and Industry (in Chicago, Illinois). Planetariums are often part of science centers or natural history museums (both the California Academy of Sciences in San Francisco and the American Museum of Natural History in New York have planetariums), but may also be freestanding, such as the Adler Planetarium in Chicago. Planetariums primarily present sky and space shows for the general public, but some also offer such nonscience events as laser light shows and concerts.

Children's Museums

The first children's museum (in the world) was the Brooklyn Children's Museum, founded in 1899 in Brooklyn, New York. Children's museums are designed to cater specifically to children (and families) and tend to be bright, colorful places with lots of interactive exhibits and activity areas. The vast majority of children's museums are exhibition and programming focused; very few maintain significant permanent collections. These museums are often centered on science or history, but in all cases children's museums emphasize the importance of informal and object-based learning. Two well-known examples are the Children's Museum of Indianapolis in Indiana (which does have a large permanent collection) and Port Discovery in Baltimore, Maryland.

Botanical Gardens, Zoos, and Aquariums

Although you may not at first think of institutions exhibiting live animals and plants as museums, they do maintain and interpret collections (and the American Alliance of Museums considers them to be museums). Because botanical gardens, zoos, and aquariums (Figure 5.3) deal with live

Figure 5.3   A museum visitor at an aquarium. Photo by authors.

organisms, their standards for collections care and the way their collections are managed are distinct from institutions with nonliving collections. In addition to collecting, caring for, and interpreting collections, these institutions sometimes also have research functions that are similar to those in other museums. For example, the Monterey Bay Aquarium (in Monterey, California) is involved in marine research and conservation work.

REALITY CHECK

Collections That Bite

Although as an undergraduate I worked in a natural history museum, I began my professional career at the Fort Worth (Texas) Zoological Park as a reptile keeper. I found a lot of similarities between the two types of institutions in the way the collections were managed, how individual specimens were tracked, and the emphasis on good record keeping. One big difference was that in the natural history museum, I didn't have to worry about one of the specimens biting and killing me. When I left the zoo for a job in a natural history museum, one of my colleagues said, "So you have decided to move from the living zoo to the dead zoo, have you?" (JES)

Small, Medium, and Large Museums

A common means of classification for museums is by size, but there are no standards for what constitutes large versus small. Size may refer to the museum's budget, the number of objects in the collection, the number of staff members, or the physical footprint of the institution. The Accreditation Committee of the American Alliance of Museums classifies museums by size based on the institution's annual budget, using the following categories:

Less than $350,000

$350,000 to $499,000

$500,000 to $999,000

$1,000,000 to $2,999,999

$3,000,000 to $4,999,999

$5,000,000 to $14,999,999

More than $15,000,000

A problem with classification by budget size is that far more than half of U.S. museums are in the first category (budgets of less than $350,000). Another problem is that a mere budget number does not tell us much about the museum, because ultimately the quality of the collection (meaning what is in it, the level of documentation, and how well it is interpreted) is more important than the number of objects in the collection or the size of the budget. A museum with a large budget may be poorly managed, while a museum with a small budget may be managed expertly. However, budget categories may be useful if we also consider factors such as the number and nature of objects in the collection, the number of staff members and how well they perform their jobs, the size of the museum audience and how well the audience is served, etc. The size of a museum alone—however it is measured—does not tell us how good a museum is. A large museum may fall far short of achieving its mission, while a small museum may be excellent. As discussed in Chapter 7, the most significant distinction concerning the size of the museum is how it affects the roles of museum staff. Most employees of small museums perform a greater variety of tasks than employees of large museums, and this affects the museum system in numerous ways.

Regional Museums: Local, State, and National

Most museums in the United States are local institutions, meaning they are locally owned and operated, often by a city or county government or a local nonprofit organization, and serve a primarily local audience. Local museums may interpret the history, cultures, or natural history of a neighborhood, city, county, state, or region (see, e.g., Figure 5.4).

State museums, as their name implies, are typically owned and run by a state government and may interpret the history, cultures, or natural history of a state. For example, the growth of the Kansas Museum of History in Topeka has followed a fairly typical pattern for a state museum. The museum itself is part of the Kansas Historical Society, which was founded by a group of newspaper editors in 1875 to collect newspapers and manuscripts related to Kansas state history. As the society grew, it became the official repository of state records, and it is now a state agency that operates several historical sites, the state archives, the state historic preservation office, and the museum that interprets the history of the state of Kansas. Another example is the State Museum of Pennsylvania in Harrisburg, created in 1905, which became part of the Pennsylvania Historical and Museum Commission

Figure 5.4 Entrance to Tiger Legacy at the Massillon Museum, an exhibit produced by the Massillon Museum in collaboration with Kent State University photojournalism professors and students to document the culture and traditions of the Massillon Tigers high school football team. Photo courtesy of the Massillon Museum.

in 1945 and now includes a planetarium and exhibits that interpret both the cultural and natural history of Pennsylvania.

National museums are those owned and operated by a national government and may interpret history, cultures, and natural history within a country. As discussed in Chapter 2, many museums that were started by colonial governments became significant national museums as countries gained their independence. For example, the Batavia Society of Arts and Science, founded as a colonial institution in 1778, is now the Central Museum of Indonesian Culture. The national museum of the United States is the Smithsonian Institution, which was established by the U.S. Congress in 1846 with a bequest from a British citizen named James Smithson. Initially a natural history museum, the Smithsonian has now grown into a complex of nineteen museums (including museums of natural history, art, history, air and space, Native Americans, African American history and culture, a postal museum, the Anacostia Community Museum, and the National Zoological Park).

Ecomuseums

One of the newest types of museums is the ecomuseum, a concept developed by two French museologists, Hugues de Varine (b. 1935) and George Rivière (1897–1985), in 1971. Varine and Rivière kept their definition of an ecomuseum intentionally vague, intending it as a concept rather than a category. The intention was not to replace the traditional concept of a museum, but rather to broaden it. Ecomuseums interpret not just an event, a place, or a culture, but an entire community, including its past and present. One description of an ecomuseum is an institution that manages heritage in a sustainable environment. An ecomuseum is designed around a community in order to combine both natural heritage and cultural heritage. What constitutes a collection in an ecomuseum may extend to the entire museum environment and thus include artifacts, buildings, and the in situ natural surroundings. For example, a traditional museum could be considered to be a building with collections in it (see Figure 5.5), while an ecomuseum is heritage preserved in situ (heritage in this sense includes cultural practices as well as material culture), such as the Hokkaido Historic Village in Sapporo, Japan. What distinguishes ecomuseums from interpreted historical sites is the ecomuseum's inclusion of a sustainable community and its surrounding environment. Ecomuseums have proven to be popular in many places in Europe, appearing first in Scandinavia and Portugal; in Canada; and in much of the developing world. There are several hundred places around the world that define themselves as ecomuseums.

Virtual Museums

Whether or not virtual museums should be included in the definition of museum is a controversial subject among museum professionals and museum studies scholars. Virtual museums exist only in cyberspace. A virtual museum does not have a physical presence; that is, it has no physical collection, no building, and no spaces with exhibits to walk through. Most virtual museums are based on real, physical collection objects, but some collect only concepts or ideas. The Virtual Museum of Japanese Art is a good example of such an enterprise. Some people consider virtual museums to be valid as museums because of their potential role in the repatriation of cultural knowledge through digitized collections and collection information, and

Figure 5.5   The Tenement Museum in New York, New York. Photo by authors.

because virtual museums can promote the sharing of information around the world. Virtual museums do provide access to information, an important contribution of museums to society, but whether they can provide meaning to visitors is another question, because the visitors are not interacting with actual objects.

A few years ago there was concern within the museum community that physical museums might be replaced by virtual museums. Despite the increasing number of virtual museums and virtual exhibits hosted by physical museums, this fear has not been realized. In fact, the data show that virtual museums and virtual museum exhibits do not cause a decrease in museum attendance, which shows that the two species can coexist successfully. Evidence shows that a virtual presence in cyberspace leads to an increased awareness of the physical museum and increased attendance. Most likely, museums will continue to exist within physical public buildings, but with growing augmentation by virtual media networks.

References

Alexander, Edward Porter, and Mary Alexander. 2008. *Museums in Motion: An Introduction to the History and Functions of Museums*. 2nd. ed. Lanham, MD: AltaMira Press.

American Alliance of Museums. n.d. "Accreditation." http://www.aam-us.org/resources/assessment-programs/accreditation.

American Alliance of Museums. N.D. Museum Facts. http://www.aam-us.org/about-museums/museum-facts.

Bell, Ford W. 2012. *How are Museums Supported Financially in the United States?* Washington, DC: United States Department of State Bureau of International Information Programs.

Burcaw, G. Ellis. 1997. *Introduction to Museum Work*. 3rd ed. Walnut Creek, CA: Altamira Press.

Davis, Peter. 1999. *Ecomuseums: A Sense of Place*. London: Leicester University Press.

Heritage Preservation. 2005. *A Public Trust at Risk: The Heritage Health Index Report on the State of America's Collections*. Washington, DC: Heritage Preservation.

Institute of Museum and Library Services. n.d. "Distribution of Museums by Discipline, FY 2014." http://www.imls.gov/assets/1/AssetManager/MUDF_Type Dist_2014q3.pdf.

Weschler, Lawrence. 1995. *Mr. Wilson's Cabinet of Wonder: Pronged Ants, Horned Humans, Mice on Toast, and Other Marvels of Jurassic Technology*. New York: Pantheon Books.

6

The Meaningful Physical Resource

Introduction

Human beings have used objects and have been immersed in a world surrounded by objects throughout their entire existence; it is, in fact, part of what has defined "human," starting with their early ancestors. For example, *Homo habilis*, long thought to be an early human ancestor, means "skillful man"; the name was chosen because the discoverers of the fossil remains believed that *Homo habilis* was the maker of the many stone tools found in the vicinity. Throughout their evolutionary history, humans have become increasingly better at modifying and shaping the world around them, thereby creating, naming, designating, and manipulating an environment full of objects. The entire history of human evolution is intertwined with the use of objects.

What Is the Meaningful Physical Resource in the Museum?

The meaningful physical resource in the museum—the object, or document—is dense with complexity. Museum collections are not simply accumulations of things. They are composed of objects that are meaningful representations of another reality (some time, place, or person) that are intentionally collected, organized, cared for, and interpreted. Objects are central to what museums offer and give museums a unique place in society as the keepers of physical bits of the world—past and present—and they are potentially the sources of deep meaning and personal sense-making. The following discussion breaks down further the phrase, *meaningful physical resource* to parse out what is entailed in this seemingly simple description.

The Physical

Thus far, it has been determined that one important aspect of defining a museum is its meaningful *physical* resource, but what does this entail? In this book (and in the museum), an object is a physical thing, a

Table 6.1 Names of the Components of Collections

Term	Definition and Comments
Article	A distinct section of a written document; a member of a class of things
Artifact	Something made, modified, or used by a human being
Element	A constituent part of a whole; a member of a set (all collections are sets of things [Simmons and Muñoz-Saba 2003])
Item	A statement or maxim; a saying with a particular bearing; a unit included in an enumeration or sum total
Material	Relating to, consisting of, or derived from matter (e.g., fossil material)
Object	Something placed before the eyes; something capable of being seen, touched, or otherwise sensed; a material thing
Piece	A part of a whole
Specimen	A representative part of a whole, or a means of discovering or finding out; an experiment, a pattern, or model
Thing	A spatial entity, an inanimate object.
Work or work of art	Something produced by creative effort; an artistic production

Based on Simmons 2006b.

three-dimensional entity that takes up space. Other descriptors used for physical entities in the museum context may include artifact, specimen, item, and material culture—each of these has a slightly different meaning, but all refer to objects. Table 6.1 provides definitions of many of these terms as used in different museal institutions.

Although each of these words has its own particular meaning, they all describe three-dimensional, physical things that can be held, touched, used, and seen. In this book, the word *object* is used to refer to the physical entities in museum collections—the meaningful physical resource—unless a more precise word is appropriate.

No matter what it is called, the physical object brings materiality to the museum experience; the undeniable physicality of the object is always present. When one encounters an object, its physical presence can be experienced, and therefore the object provides some information through the user's senses: size, shape, color, texture, etc. All humans experience objects through their senses, albeit in varying ways and through varying lenses unique to each individual. Objects are encountered as much by the body as by the mind, and it is not possible to split the relationship between the senses and cognitive processes, because both are required to interpret objects.

The Meaningful

How is it that objects are, or become, *meaningful*? As ubiquitous elements of an everyday landscape, objects are often taken for granted, but in fact, a single object can be very complicated. Objects are polysemic, which means they can have many meanings, and those meanings can change in different situations and contexts. Object meanings are partly constructed from the viewer's position. One person, at a specific time, in a particular culture, with a certain set of knowledge, is what determines how that object is deciphered in that moment. A common adage in museum work states that "objects speak for themselves." This is a problematic representation, because it anthropomorphizes objects and puts them on the same level as humans, presuming that objects have some kind of innate agency. Even though they are created or interpreted by humans, objects cannot speak for themselves, although they do hold great power and are incredibly important vessels for communicating ideas. In actuality, objects only communicate *through* people. Even with a physical presence, it is only through a person's understanding and prior experience of the world that an object can "speak." Objects do not communicate without someone to communicate with; thus the meanings of an object are the result of a symbiotic relationship between a person and that object. The person may be a curator, a collection manager, a museum educator, a visitor, or all of the above. Meaning is found neither entirely in the viewer nor entirely in the object; it is dialogic, which is to say, meaning is produced through a dialog between the viewer and the object (Hooper-Greenhill 2000).

Regarding this relationship, there are certain facts about objects and people that are important to understand. Both objects and people have life histories. Both have unique pasts. A mass-produced object, even if it appears identical to other objects manufactured at the same time, has its own history of ownership and use, compared to the other objects that, on the surface, look exactly the same. Likewise, different individuals bring with them unique experiences and knowledge that affect how they interact with an object in a museum exhibit.

REALITY CHECK

A Box of Marbles

Given two seemingly identical objects, why does one have greater value than another? I keep a small box of marbles on the bookshelf in my office. The marbles look pretty much alike. All are glass, all are old, and all are chipped. However, one of those marbles carries much more meaning for me than the others because it belonged to my father when he was a boy. The others are just marbles I dug up while working in the garden. It is the documented history of the marble that my father used to play with that gives it a value the others lack. It has a location and ownership history, historical affiliation, and personal connections that I use to make my own meaning for the object. (JES)

Back to the "M Words"

In Chapter 1 the concepts surrounding the term *museal* were discussed. Stransky (in Maroević 1998), the originator of the term, said that the museum object is to be considered a *document* of the reality of the time from which it was taken. Throughout its life, the object accumulates a certain amount of data that can be interpreted by museum users and workers. In this sense, a museum object carries data from two realities, its original reality and the museum reality. Van Mensch (1992) builds on this by proposing that an open approach to understanding and using museum objects should be adopted by museologists, instead of a closed disciplinary approach that limits perspective to only one aspect of the object. Van Mensch's perspective, which sees the object as a limitless source of information—as a data carrier—is an essential concept for museum studies.

Objects in a museum are endowed with museality and is called musealia (the museum objects themselves). A museal object is one that has been taken from some reality, for example, a shell bead that was collected from a Plains Woodland house site, to represent this original reality in the new context of the museum. The museality of the shell bead in the museum exists because it stands as evidence of the time in which the object originated. For example, the shell bead from the Plains Woodland house was made from a freshwater mussel. The mussel was once alive; a complex, resilient lining (called the nacre or mother-of-pearl) was deposited on the inside of the shell. That is one reality. A few thousand years ago, an American Indian picked up the mussel, drilled the bead from the nacre, polished it, and placed it on a string. The bead may have been used by the person who made it, or perhaps traded to other Native Americans, before it became buried in a Plains Woodland house. This is another reality (or set of realities). Eventually the bead was excavated by an archaeologist and placed in a museum collection. As a musealized object, the shell bead represents the reality of the freshwater river where the mussel grew, the culture of the American Indian craftsman who carved the nacre from the mussel, and the culture that used the bead in a Plains Woodland house. When something is musealized, it is transformed into a *representative* of some time, place, context, or person. The museum serves as a medium for the transmission of information from the past to the present, and the present to the future. Of course the transformation from original use object to a musealized object is not limited to museums. We often find musealized things in other contexts, such as antique malls, parks, and festivals. Maroević (1998) points out that castles, churches, and archaeological sites are in situ examples of musealized things. What is different in a museum is the active, intentional communication and interpretation of the object. From iconic objects such as Abraham Lincoln's stovepipe hat to everyday objects such as a mid-twentieth-century rolling pin, the process of musealization can occur with any object. Museality is directly linked to physicality; that is, only physical things can be musealized.

In his consideration of museality, Maroević introduced the concept of "museal indefiniteness," which describes the fact that everything about an object can never be known in its entirety. Imagine all the information ever associated with a single object over its entire existence. Although every bit of this information can never be recovered, museum researchers can constantly learn more about the object, decreasing its museal indefiniteness while increasing its museal definiteness. For example, a paleontologist finds a mammoth tooth in Nebraska and brings it to a museum. Over time, the tooth is studied by paleontologists, who gradually learn more about the mammoth. They determine that the tooth was from a young mammoth (because of its size), discover what it ate (from the remains of vegetation caught between the plates of the tooth), figure out the time that it lived (from chemical analysis of the tooth and the context it was found in) and how the young mammoth died (because the tooth was found buried in volcanic ash). But no matter how much the tooth is studied, the paleontologists will never learn everything about it. In other words, defining the content of musealia (the mammoth tooth) is a communication process in which the field of museal indefiniteness of the object decreases with the continued accumulation of information about it.

What Is a Collection?

Musealized objects are components of museum collections. At this point, it is important to stop and ask, "What is a collection?" As touched upon in Chapter 2, the difference between an accumulation of objects and a collection is that an accumulation occurs by chance, but a collection is assembled on purpose. Because a collection is assembled on purpose, it is organized in some way, which means that it has some kind of order (otherwise it wouldn't and couldn't be organized). The order may make sense only to the collector; but no matter, a collection has order. In *Museums, Objects and Collections* (1993), Susan Pearce pointed out that all collections have three things in common:

1. They are made up of objects.

2. The objects come to us from the past.

3. They have been assembled with some degree of intention (however slight) by an owner or curator who believed that the whole was somehow more than the sum of its parts.

Many definitions of collections are found in the museum literature, but there seems to be little agreement around any single one. For example, museum collections have been defined as the objects in a museum's care (Case 1988), as a group of objects with like characteristics and a common association (Society for the Preservation of Natural History Collections 1994), and as objects acquired and preserved because they have potential value to the museum (Burcaw 1997).

What is amiss in these definitions of *collection* is that they fail to distinguish the unique qualities of museum collections, the qualities that separate them from other kinds of collections of objects. Nicholson and Williams (2002) proposed a definition of museum collections that differentiates them from other kinds of collections:

- Collections consist of more than one object.

- The objects have order and organization.

- The objects are valued by people.

- The objects are collected with the intent to preserve them over time.

- Collections serve the institutional mission and goals.

- The integrity of the object and its associated information are paramount.

- Collections are maintained in adherence to professional standards.

What this definition does is to distinguish musealia (the meaningful physical resource, the objects in museum collections) from other objects by defining what makes objects in museum collections different from other objects.

Paradigm Shifts:
From Object to Visitor to Document

A major trend in American museums beginning in the late twentieth century was the shift toward an emphasis on the museum visitor—and away from the object or collection. For too long, museum staff had not involved their audiences in the process of interpretation. Museums functioned as authoritative knowledge centers in which visitors were positioned to learn *from*, not *with*. Conn (1998) called this earlier approach an "object-based epistemology," in which emphasis was on the facts and explanation of an object, and where the order and meaning of objects were *revealed to* the visitor, making interpretation a covert, closed act (Evans, Mull, and Poling 2002) in which the objects, not the text (interpretation), were presented as the source of knowledge. According to Conn, this object-based epistemology was foundational in the development of museums.

In the late twentieth century a shift to an "object-based dialogue" began that underscored the importance of a shared process in which the object, the presentation (including the people behind the creation of this presentation), and the visitors jointly participated in acts of meaning (Evans, Mull, and Poling 2002, 115). Increasingly, the visitor role became a focus, and more research developed around what visitors were learning and experiencing, yielding important insights into how museums work and what people take away from their visits. As a result of this period of development, objects moved to the background. But recent research shows that it is the visitor's interaction with the object that creates the unique experience that is today's museum.

Honing in on what makes museums unique entities in society, it is the objects that they preserve, interpret, organize, study, and share, and the human relationships formed with these objects. No other institution uses physical, material things to inspire, teach, preserve, etc., in the way museums do. Libraries do not. Archives do not. Disneyland does not. Of course there are similarities between museums and these institutions, but when it comes down to it, the meaningful physical resource is at the crux of what makes a museum a museum. The relationship between objects and people must be clear if it is claimed that this relationship is what makes museums unique. By understanding museum objects as documents—which follows— the object can be rightfully placed at the center of the museum.

From the field of document studies (related to library and information science) comes the notion of *document*. The word is derived from the Latin word *documentum*, meaning proof, pattern, or example. Beginning in the thirteenth century, early definitions of documentation described it as teaching, instruction, or informing. Only later (in the early eighteenth century) did the word document become associated with paper or other material upon which text was written. Since then, the word has become muddled and layered with many meanings, mostly in association with textual material and printed matter.

Today, documentalists—practitioners and scholars concerned with using, organizing, accessing, analyzing, and understanding documents in theory and application—use the term *document* to denote any physical information resource, any physical expression or representation of human thought (Buckland 1997), rather than limiting it to specific text-bearing, print-based media (Buckland 1991).

Documentation can refer to both the process of documenting something and the outcome of that process (Buckland 2007). Michael Buckland has called a document "any signifying thing" and "any organized physical evidence," indicating the dual nature of a document as a physical thing and its representation of something. Lund (2004) defines document as any expression of human thought that simultaneously embodies qualities of being social, physical, and mental; that is, a document has a physical dimension, serves a communicative purpose, is created within a certain community of social actors, and is useful for a certain audience (Mannheim 1952). "Madame Documentation," as Suzanne Briet became known, has contributed to document discourse the definition "any concrete or symbolic indexical sign [indice], preserved or recorded toward the ends of representing, of reconstituting, or of proving a physical or intellectual phenomenon" (Briet 2006, 10).

Just as the book, the manuscript, and the microform are physical objects that are potentially able to inform someone, museum *objects* are also potentially informative. Using the definition of a document as a physical thing that represents something to someone, a museum object is also a document. When the world is divided between all objects and museum objects, it is more obvious why museum objects are documents. Briet is credited with establishing four conditions for something to be considered a document (Buckland 1997):

1. Materiality—physical objects and physical signs only;
2. Intentionality—the object is intended to be treated as evidence;
3. Process—the object has to be made into a document; and
4. Phenomenological position—the object is perceived to be a document.

First, materiality—museum objects are physical, just as all objects are. By definition, a material entity is manifested in physical, material form. Second, intentionality—museums collect objects by seeking them or accepting offered donations. Objects are collected because museum staff has determined that in some way they are important to keep, either to help tell a story of some kind or to represent some behavior, idea, person, event, or function. Third, process—cataloging is a major part of museum work, and in the past couple of decades, serious efforts have been put into creating standards and best practices for the processing of museum objects. Other sorts of processing of museum objects include exhibition, loans, and educational use. Last, phenomenological position—intimately bound with Briet and Buckland's second criterion of intentionality—objects are perceived by museum staff and visitors as entities of evidence, or as documents (whether they use this word or not). The very fact that an object has been entered into a collection makes it a document—a concrete, symbolic, indexical sign that is preserved or recorded (cataloged, stored, cared for) with the purpose of representing, reconstituting, or proving a physical or intellectual phenomenon (research, exhibition, preservation). When a seemingly mundane object enters a museum collection, it becomes something else—a museum object; it has been musealized (Van Mensch 2004, 1992; Maroević 1998); it is a document.

The most famous example of a document from Briet is the antelope. To Briet, a wild antelope running on the savanna in its natural environment was not a document, but a captured antelope, taken to a zoo as an object of study, was a document (what she called an initial or primary document), because it became physical evidence. In addition, any materials about the antelope—photographs, written records, audio recordings—were also documents (what she called derived, or secondary documents). In Briet's (2006) own words:

> [F]or example, an antelope of a new kind has been encountered in Africa by an explorer who has succeeded in capturing an individual that is then brought back to Europe for our Botanical Garden. . . . A press release makes the event known by newspaper, by radio, and by newsreels. The discovery becomes the topic of an announcement at the Academy of Science. A professor of the Museum discusses it in his courses. The living animal is placed in a

cage and cataloged. . . . Once it is dead, it will be stuffed and preserved (in the Museum). It is loaned to an Exposition. It is played
on a soundtrack at a cinema. Its voice is recorded on a disk. The
first monograph serves to establish part of a treatise with places,
then a special encyclopedia . . . then a general encyclopedia. The
works are cataloged in a library, after having been announced at
publication. . . . The documents are recopied (drawings, watercol-
ors, paintings, statues, photos, films, microfilms), then selected,
analyzed, described, translated. . . . The cataloged antelope is an
initial document and the other documents are secondary or derived. (2006, 10)

The concept of document is important for understanding the museum
system and the museum object in both library and information science and
museum studies. It opens up a broad perspective and offers a new understanding of the human relationship with information. Museum objects, as
musealia, become documents by the associations they reflect; they have
many stories to tell. While museum workers have traditionally not seen
museum objects as "documents," they understand, perhaps more than
most, that museum objects are involved in this kind of representation and
communication.

The Document-Centered Museum

In this book, today's museum is conceptualized to be a document-
centered institution. What this means is that everything that museums
do comes back to documents and documentation—that is, objects and how
they are interpreted, classified, preserved, and experienced. The document-
centered museum is not the same as Conn's object-based epistemology, in
which all understanding is derived from the object. The document, being
a social, physical, and mental entity, is more than this. It is a meaningful
representation of some time, place, or being, and is perceived in a multitude
of ways by different viewers. Document centered means that documents are
the pivot point for all activities, meanings, and purposes in the museum
(see Figure 6.1). Recall the feedback loops mentioned in previous chapters.
The document and all the elements of the museum form connections to each
other and back again. This is a dynamic and holistic view of the museum that
acknowledges what makes museums unique is the document—the physical
thing that signifies—and its relationship within networks of people.

Person-Document Transaction

In the document-centered museum, the relationship between a person
(either a worker or a visitor) and an object is essential. There is something
special about the encounter between a person and a physical thing that is
not the same as when the object sits alone or when the person hasn't yet encountered it. When the two meet, an experience between them can occur, a
moment when the two merge, unite. This experience is called a transaction,
or more specifically, a person-document transaction. In the museum setting,
Wood and Latham (2013) describe this as a *unified experience*, emphasizing the fact that it is something that happens when both object and person
meet. The concept of transaction comes from the work of John Dewey, the
well-known philosopher and educational reformer of the early twentieth
century. A transaction in the museum is a unique occurrence that is central

Figure 6.1 The document-centered museum.

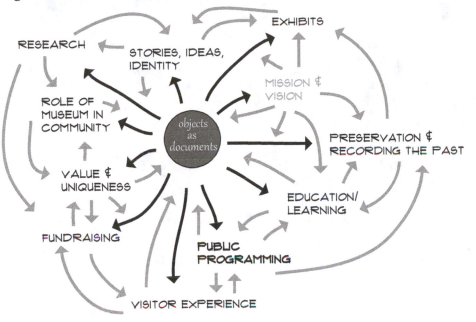

to all that is done in museums. Museums are about things (the meaningful physical resource) and the public (museum users), but the height of the museum experience is the coming together of these two (transaction). This is what makes museums unique institutions in society. Nowhere else can you find a place that presents real things for people to encounter other than museums and related institutions (e.g., national parks and monuments). The relationship between a person and a document is central to all museum work and experience. Museum workers might ask themselves why they do what they do. Why catalog this object? Why make a mount for this exhibit? Why create brochures for the museum? Why teach schoolchildren about this topic? In all of these cases, it is the transaction that happens between a person and an object. It is similar for the visitor: Why would anyone come to a museum? What are people coming to see that they can't see online or in a book? Of course, there are many reasons given by visitors, such as wanting to learn, to be with family, to feel cultured, and so forth, but they can do these things in other ways, such as by watching a documentary, visiting Disneyland, or going to an opera. What makes the museum experience unique is the immersion in an environment containing physical objects (documents) that have a presence and how that makes the visitor feel. Whether or not a person actually focuses on a single object or a whole exhibit, there is an effect that is felt from being in the presence of musealized things.

References

Briet, Suzanne. 2006. *What Is Documentation? English Translation of the Classic French Text*. Translated by R. E. Day and L. Martinet. Lanham, MD: Scarecrow Press.

Buckland, Michael K. 1991a. "Information as Thing." *Journal of the American Society for Information Science* 42, no. 5: 351–360.

Buckland, Michael K. 1991b. "Information Retrieval of More Than Text." *Journal of the American Society for Information Science* 42, no. 8: 586–588.

Buckland, Michael K. 1997. "What Is a 'Document'?" *Journal of the American Society for Information Science* 48, no. 9:804–809.

Buckland, Michael K. 2007. "Northern Light: Fresh Insights into Enduring Concerns." In *A Document (Re)turn: Contributions from a Research Field in Transition*, edited by Roswitha Skare, Niels Windfield Lund, and Andreas Vårheim, 327–334. Frankfurt am Main: Peter Lang.

Burcaw, G. Ellis. 1997. *Introduction to Museum Work*. 3rd ed. Walnut Creek, CA: Altamira Press.

Case, Mary. 1988. *Registrars on Record: Essays on Museum Collections Management*. Washington DC: Registrars Committee of the American Association of Museums.

Conn, Steven. 1998. *Museums and American Intellectual Life, 1876–1926*. Chicago: University of Chicago Press.

Dewey, John, and Arthur Bentley. 1949. *Knowing and the Known*. Boston: Beacon Press.

Evans, E. Margaret, Melinda S. Mull, and Devereaux A. Poling. 2002. "The Authentic Object? A Child's-eye View." In *Perspectives on Object-Centered Learning in Museums*, edited by Scott G. Paris, 55–77. Mahwah, NJ: Lawrence Erlbaum Associates.

Hodder, Ian. 2012. *Entangled: An Archaeology of the Relationships between Humans and Things*. Malden, MA: Wiley-Blackwell.

Hooper-Greenhill, Eilean. 2000. *Museums and the Interpretation of Visual Culture*. London: Routledge.

Latham, Kiersten F. 2009. "Numinous Experiences with Museum Objects." PhD diss., Emporia State University.

Lund, Neils Windfeld. n.d. "Documentation in a Complementary Perspective." http://scholar.google.com/citations?view_op=view_citation&hl=en&user=zFJjPJcAAAAJ&citation_for_view=zFJjPJcAAAAJ:u-x6o8ySG0sC.

MacGregor, Neal. 2010. *A History of the World in 100 Objects*. New York: Viking.

Mannheim, Karl. 1952. *Essays on the Sociology of Knowledge*. New York: Oxford University Press.

Maroević, Ivo. 1998. *Introduction to Museology: The European Approach*. Munich: C. Müller-Straten.

Nicholson, E. G., and S. L. Williams. 2002. "Developing a Working Definition for the Museum Collection." *Inside Line* (Fall): 1–4.

Pearce, Susan M. 1993. *Museums, Objects and Collections: A Cultural Study*. Washington, DC: Smithsonian Institution Press.

Simmons, John E. 2006a. *Things Great and Small: Collections Management Policies*. Washington DC: American Association of Museums.

Simmons, John E. 2006b. "Museum Studies Programs in North America." In *Museum Studies: Perspectives and Innovations*, edited by Stephen L. Williams and Catharine A. Hawks, 113–128. Washington, DC: Society for the Preservation of Natural History Collections.

Simmons, John E., and Yaneth Muñoz-Saba. 2003. "The Theoretical Bases of Collections Management." *Collection Forum* 18, nos. 1–2: 38–49.

Society for the Preservation of Natural History Collections. 1994. "Guidelines for the Care of Natural History Collections," *Collection Forum* 10, no. 1: 32–40.

Van Mensch, Peter. 1992. "Towards a Methodology of Museology." PhD diss., University of Zagreb, http://www.muzeologie.net/downloads/mat_lit/mensch_phd.pdf.

Van Mensch, Peter. 2004. "Museology and Management: Enemies or Friends? Current Tendencies in Theoretical Museology and Museum Management in Europe." In *Museum Management in the 21st Century*, edited by E. Mizushima, 3–19. Tokyo: Museum Management Academy.

Wood, Elizabeth, and Kiersten F. Latham. 2013. *The Objects of Experience. Transforming Visitor-Object Encounters in Museums*. Walnut Creek, CA: Left Coast Press.

Section Four
Who

7

Museum Workers

Early Development of Museum Work

The tasks performed by the people who work in museums have evolved enormously since the emergence of the first museums. As discussed in Chapter 2, modern museums grew out of the private cabinets of curiosities of the Renaissance. Although most of the owners of the cabinets are known individuals, not much is known about the people who assisted them in accumulating and caring for their collections; however, there are a few tantalizing glimpses into how some of these cabinets were run (Findlen 1994). For example, a woodcut prepared in 1599 shows Ferrante Imperato (1525–1625), an apothecary and collector, giving a tour of his private cabinet of curiosities (this image can easily be found by searching for "Ferrante Imperato" on the Web and is considered to be the first illustration of a museum). In the woodcut, Imperato and his guests are standing in a room with a high ceiling. The room is lined with shelves and cabinets; stuffed and dried animals are suspended from the ceiling itself, and Imperato is using a long stick to point to some of these trophies. What is not shown in this woodcut are the assistants who probably prepared the specimens and arranged the objects in the room under Imperato's direction. By contrast, an etching published in 1677 shows Ferdinando Cospi (1606–1686) standing amid his collection while the museum caretaker or *custode del museo*, a dwarf named Sebastiano Biavati, cleans an object on a shelf. With the exception of Biavati, the assistants who toiled in early modern museums are rarely mentioned in the published descriptions of the museums. Biavati was in the unusual position of being both an assistant and, in a way, part of the collection.

In another example, a copperplate illustration from the 1706 catalog of Levin Vincent's museum (see Figure 7.1), the Wondertoonel der Natur (Theater of Nature's Marvels), shows visitors to the museum along with at least one assistant. Vincent (1658–1727) was a cloth merchant in Amsterdam who used his wealth to create a very large cabinet of curiosities and published the catalog of his collections. Most of the visitors depicted in the illustration are very well dressed and therefore can be identified as members of the same socioeconomic class as Vincent himself; but there is one young assistant in the lower right corner of the image, dressed in much less elegant clothing, who appears to be helping some visitors locate certain objects.

Figure 7.1   Vincent's museum, 1706.

Museum budget records from the 1800s show assistants on the payroll of many institutions, but they do not tell us anything about the training of these individuals or what specific tasks they performed. In 1900 the English Egyptologist William Flinders Matthew Petrie proposed building a large common collections storage facility for London museums and suggested that the staff for the facility would need only minimal training to catalog, house, and care for the collections under the direction of a few expert curators (Petrie 1900; Podgomy 2012). To speed up the slow process of cataloging collections, Petrie recommended the use of a then-new technology—close-up, high-resolution, black-and-white photography—to replace detailed object descriptions. Petrie did not anticipate the greater level of content and collections management expertise that is common in museums today, although he was correct in his prediction that museums of the future would embrace many forms of technology to address their collections cataloging and care problems.

By the early twentieth century museum workers in the United States were becoming more specialized and needed more training. For example, the first full-time museum educators, hired around the time of World War I, were schoolteachers. John Cotton Dana, the director of the Newark Museum in Newark, New Jersey, was a pioneer in developing museum education as a profession. Dana believed that the presence of museum educators changed museums from what he called "grazing museums" to "institutes of visual instruction." During the 1920s and 1930s the first research studies on museum education were published, leading to further specialization of museum educators. In 1932 only 15 percent of museums in the United States had educational programs, but by 1960 some 79 percent of museums had them (Roberts 1997). The people hired as curators in large museums during this time were usually specialists in academic subjects such as anthropology, art history, biology, or history, with advanced degrees in their field of study.

Many exhibit staff members were recruited for their backgrounds in graphic arts or fine arts. The title of registrar was first used in museums in the late 1800s and became increasingly common after 1900.

Throughout the twentieth century museum jobs became professionalized, and more new titles appeared, including exhibition developer, collection manager, and visitor services manager. One indication of the rapid professionalization of the museum field was the formation of professional associations for museum workers, beginning with the Museums Association, founded in the United Kingdom in 1889. The American Association of Museums, now American Alliance of Museums (AAM), was founded in 1906, and its first periodic publication, *Museum Work* (later called *Museum News*, now *Museum*), began publication in 1918. The American Historical Association started in 1884, and the American Association for State and Local History (AASLH) in 1940. The International Council of Museums (ICOM) was founded in 1946. Although all possible positions in today's museum system are not covered, a variety of tasks and titles currently found in museums are discussed in more detail below.

Training and Preparation for Museum Work

Even though many museum staff members from the late 1800s onward were professionally trained (e.g., as accountants, artists, schoolteachers, and academic discipline experts), formal training in museum studies has only been available for a little more than a hundred years, and most university-based museum studies programs are less than forty years old. The reason it has taken so long for formal museum studies training programs to develop is due, in large part, to the failure of many in the museum profession to recognize the need for specialized training as well as a lack of agreement on what museum studies programs should teach. For many years preparation for a museum career was considered to be nothing more than a combination of a discipline degree (e.g., anthropology or history) or a technical degree (e.g., accounting, teaching) and on-the-job experience in museums. This system produced competent museum workers, but did not produce museologists with a good understanding of museum philosophy, techniques, and museum theory, all of which are necessary for the progress of the profession (Simmons 2006).

The first formal training program in the United States for museum professionals was started in 1908 by Sarah Yorke Stevenson at the Pennsylvania Museum and School of Industrial Art in Philadelphia, followed by programs at Wellesley College in 1910, the University of Iowa in 1911, Harvard in 1921, and at the Newark Museum in 1925. Despite this beginning, it was not until the 1970s that graduate programs in museum studies began to proliferate. Today a variety of accredited master's degree programs in museum studies, both residential and online, are available, as well as graduate certificate programs in various aspects of museum studies and several certificate programs not affiliated with universities.

Workers, Departments, and the Tasks to Be Done

There are many tasks to be done in any museum. In larger museums, the staff tends to be more specialized, and each person performs fewer tasks more often. In smaller museums the staff is more generalized, and each person performs a greater number of tasks but each less often. Because most museum professionals work in smaller museums and must perform multiple tasks, job titles are rarely a reliable guide to describing what responsibilities the job includes. Furthermore, both societal expectations of museums and economic considerations are forcing most museums to find new ways to do more with less. As museum collections grow ever larger, the already skewed ratio of the number of trained collections care staff, for example, to the number of objects to be cared for will continue to be lopsided. In the future most museum professionals can expect to be called upon to perform a greater variety of tasks than their predecessors. Another recent trend in museum work is the use of consultants. Because the number of employees of any museum is constrained by budget limitations, some museum tasks that used to be done in-house are now done by outside consultants on a contractual basis, particularly tasks such as exhibit development and installation, Web design, conservation of objects, evaluation, and fund-raising.

A Word about Titles . . .

The way tasks are divided among staff members varies from one museum to another, depending on the museum size, organization, the content of the collection, museum mission, and so forth. For purposes of discussion, the various tasks are described here under the general job title of the person who performs them, but in practice most museum professionals have blended jobs. Furthermore, the same job title may mean something very different from one museum to another, particularly the title *curator*, as discussed below. Applicants looking for a museum job should read the job description responsibilities carefully to understand exactly what the person hired will be expected to do. People looking for a museum job must be careful not to be misled by the job title and look for what they want to do rather than for the title they think they should have. The jobs found in administration, collections, conservation, education, exhibition, public relations, security, maintenance, visitor services, and research are described below using traditional job titles, but recall that the museum system is intricately interconnected and not always hierarchical, and some museums use only a few of the titles from this list. For example, rarely will you find a development officer in a small museum, but you can almost always find a director.

Administration

Director

Museum directors are administrators who bear the ultimate responsibility for how the museum operates. In some museums, particularly in large institutions, the director may have the title chief executive officer (CEO). In almost all museums, the director reports to either a board of trustees or a board of directors, or to some government agency. In many university museums, the director reports to a department chair, dean, university president, or equivalent. Modern museum directors spend a surprising amount of their time fund-raising for their museums by visiting potential donors, appealing to granting agencies, and working with potential corporate sponsors. Directors must have good management skills (both personnel and financial), be good planners and communicators, and have polished diplomatic skills.

They are usually the crucial communication link between the board or other governance structure of the museum and the staff. In larger museums, directors do not usually directly supervise all staff members, so they depend on a reliable network of museum professionals or staff to carry out the mission of the museum.

Development Officer

Development is the crucial fund-raising work that must be conducted to raise money in support of the museum's mission. While development officers are usually not required to have particular museum expertise, the better they understand museums, the more effective they can be in working with potential donors. Development staff members, often called development officers, typically have backgrounds in finance, accounting, or business, and most have very good social skills, as well as excellent communication skills. It is important for development personnel to understand such issues as the kinds of gifts that museums accept, what the museum needs to support its mission, and how the museum collection should grow and develop. Development officers work with donors, grant writers, and funding agencies to help the museum meet its financial goals.

Grant Writer

Grant writing is a specialized form of expository writing. Grant writers must be attentive to detail and able to carefully follow directions in grant preparation, but must also be persuasive in the way they present the museum's needs. Although a degree in museum studies is rarely a requirement for grant writers, a good understanding of museum functions (and the system) will help a grant writer be much more effective. Grant writers are expected to be familiar with a variety of foundation and governmental grant sources and what the requirements and deadlines are for each type of grant, and to have a demonstrable record of success in grant writing. A grant writer may not be on permanent staff, but may be hired as a temporary worker or consultant.

Web Designer

Good Web design is often overlooked by other museum personnel, but many museum visitors' first introduction to museums is through their Web sites, and thus a well-designed site is critical. Web designers should have a background in information technology and design. Although a degree in museum studies is not frequently a requirement for a Web designer, individuals who understand the complexity of museums will be able to produce the best products for the museum.

Attorney

Museum law is a rare specialty among lawyers, but an extremely valuable one for a museum. Museum law covers a range of topics, from legal issues affecting nonprofits to copyright law to international laws and conventions on the movement of cultural property, plants, and wildlife. Most museums hire lawyers only when necessary instead of keeping a lawyer on staff. Museum lawyers usually have a doctor of jurisprudence (JD) degree and are members of the state bar.

Financial Officer

A museum financial officer may be required to have a degree in accounting or business, or be a certified public accountant (CPA), depending on the size and complexity of the museum. Financial officers are responsible for budgeting and managing the museum's accounts and payroll. In an institution as complex as a large museum, managing finances can become very complicated. Not only do financial officers have to deal with typical business expenses, they also have to understand how people do field work, design and construct exhibits, the vagaries of the commercial market in museum objects, and have a keen understanding of the laws and regulations that affect nonprofit institutions.

Human Resources Officer

The tasks of a human resources officer are not all that different in museums than they are in other organizations, except that in a museum, the human resources officer will probably have to deal with a much bigger variety of employment responsibilities among the staff. Human resource officers are usually required to have a degree in personnel management or business.

Membership Director

Many museums depend on their members for support, so the position of membership director is critical. The membership director or coordinator takes the lead in designing the membership program, developing benefits and activities for members, recruiting members, and often working closely with the volunteer coordinator and development staff. In effect, the membership director plays a key role in interpreting the museum to its most loyal audience. Most membership directors have good interpersonal skills and formal training in public relations, marketing, or museum studies.

Volunteers

Volunteers play important roles in many museums, and some small museums are entirely volunteer run with no paid employees. They are typically interested individuals who have undergone some degree of training, if only through orientation in the museum where they participate. Volunteers are most often found working at the public interfaces of the museum, such as information desks and special events, but may also serve as tour guides, educators, collection or research assistants, or even curators. It is not uncommon for professional scientists or scholars to continue their research work on a volunteer basis in a museum after they retire. Some museums distinguish docents, who serve primarily in an educational role, from other volunteers, but in other museums all volunteers may be called docents or just volunteers.

Volunteer or Docent Coordinator

Benjamin Ives Gilman (1852–1933), director of the Boston Museum of Fine Arts from 1893 to 1925, introduced the word *docent* to museums. The root of docent is the Latin word *docēre*, which means to teach. In the United States a docent is a trained volunteer who serves as a museum guide or instructor, or performs other duties related to public service. Some museums have very extensive docent programs and offer formal training for their docents. Some small museums are mostly volunteer run and thus depend on the loyalty, goodwill, and dedication of their docents to function. It is the job of the docent coordinator to recruit, train, supervise, and inspire the docents. A docent coordinator must have good interpersonal skills and might have a formal background in education. In some cases, museums have volunteers who do work beyond that of the docent, and a volunteer manager can help coordinate their schedules with those of the museum staff and programs.

Collections

Archivist

Archival work is primarily focused on the organization, indexing, classification, storage, and retrieval of manuscripts and records. Although traditional archives have consisted mainly of paper-based documents, modern archives also contain information stored on other media, including film, tape, and digital formats. Digital preservation is becoming an important skill set for all archivists. Museum archivists primarily work with records that are used in support of the collections and the history of the museum and its operations, but may also care for related historical collections. Currently used collections records are typically in the care of registrars and collections managers. Most archivist positions require graduate work in library and information science or history.

Collection Manager and Registrar

The professions of collection manager and registrar are very similar, and in some instances the titles are synonymous. The title *registrar* was first used in museums in the late nineteenth and early twentieth centuries to refer to museum workers who processed accessions and handled other collection-related record keeping (Figure 7.2). The title *collection manager* was first used in natural history museums in the mid-1970s. For a time, *collection manager* referred to someone working with collections and collection-related records in very large natural history or history collections, while registrar was reserved for art collections and small to medium museum collections, but these distinctions faded away by the end of the 1990s. In the business world (outside of the museum profession), a collection manager may also refer to someone in charge of debt collection. Standard preparation for museum collection manager and registrar positions is an undergraduate degree in a specialized subject such as art history, history, or natural history, and a graduate degree in museum studies or library and information science with a special emphasis in registration and collections management.

Curator

The job title *curator* is widely applied but inconsistently used. A curator may refer to a researcher, a highly specialized subject expert, or someone who cares for a collection. The word *keeper* is sometimes still used for curators with primarily collections care responsibilities. Curators who are researchers generally have a PhD in their academic specialty and conduct collections-based research, provide expert content for exhibits and educational programs, and assist with collection growth and development. Curators whose primary responsibility is collections care typically have an

Figure 7.2   Cataloging collections in an electronic database. Earth and Mineral Sciences Museum & Art Gallery, Penn State University. Photograph by the authors.

undergraduate degree in an academic subject and a master's degree in museum studies or similar degree, such as public history. In some museums, curators also perform some collection registration and cataloging tasks. Increasingly, curators are expected to come out from behind the scenes and communicate their knowledge to the public.

REALITY CHECK

Title Schmitle

A case in point about title terminology comes from one of the positions I held during my professional career working in museums. My job title was Curator of Collections. Based on our list of jobs in this chapter, that title might be a little confusing, but it was a good title for what I did, as I was both the collection manager and the curator of the collection. I certainly was not an expert in the museum's topic, space history, but I grew to know it over time. My tasks were divided between registration (in-house and loan work), collections care (Figure 7.3) and organization, and exhibition research and mountmaking. In another position, my title was Curator of Collections and Research; I was responsible for the care of a large collection of local artifacts and archives, but also worked on policy, budgeting, writing and design of in-house exhibits. In neither job—both in medium-sized museums—did I have, or was required to hold, a PhD. (KFL)

Figure 7.3   Condition reporting inside a flown Gemini spacecraft, Kansas Cosmosphere and Space Center, Hutchinson, Kansas. Photograph by authors.

Information Technologist

The information technology (IT) needs of museums can be eclectic. In addition to software and hardware to manage the budget and payroll, museum IT staff have to be familiar with collection management hardware and software, systems used in the museum store and food services, and often with design software used in exhibits. Most museum IT personnel have a degree in information technology or computer science.

Preparator

In the museum world, a preparator is someone who specializes in the packing and shipping of museum objects, and often in their installation and de-installation in the exhibit galleries. Due to the specialized nature of preparator's tasks, most preparators are trained on the job in the institution they work for, but often they have degrees in fine arts or applied arts. A title similar to preparator is also used in natural history museums for people who do very specific specimen work, such as fossil preparator.

Photographer

The position of museum photographer has changed drastically over the last fifteen years due to the introduction of digital imaging. A contemporary museum photographer must not only know how to take high-quality photographs and meet the specialized photographic needs of the collections, exhibition, marketing, and research staff, but also be adept with digital imaging technology, including scanning and 3-D imaging. In some cases the photographer needs to be familiar with copyright and licensing issues related to photographing the collections. Many museums still have large image collections in traditional film formats, including black-and-white negatives, color negatives, color slides, movie film, and video, so many museums require their photographers to know how to work with these materials as well. Most museum photographers are trained either in fine arts with a specialization in photography or as photojournalists.

Conservation

Conservator

Conservators are trained in collection and object evaluation and preservation. There are three broad types of conservation work: bench work, or work on individual objects; collection work, with a focus on collection storage environments to prevent collection deterioration; and research into conservation methodologies and techniques. Bench conservators and collection conservators typically have a master's degree in conservation science; research conservators usually have a PhD in materials science or chemistry. The work of a museum conservator will vary greatly with the type of collections and how large the museum is. In smaller and more diverse institutions, conservators tend to be generalists with an overall knowledge base in many areas, but larger institutions may hire specialized conservators such as those who work only on baroque-era paintings or in paper conservation. Most conservator positions are found in larger museums.

Conservation Technician

Conservation technicians are preservation specialists who have less extensive training and experience than conservators. They work either under the direction of a conservator or in close consultation with a conservator.

Education

Educator

Historically, many museum educators had training and often certification as classroom teachers. In response to the growth of museum education and research on informal learning, it is becoming more common to find museum educators with degrees in museum studies rather than degrees in education, but the backgrounds of museum educators remain diverse. Most museum educators today are trained in learning theory and advocate for visitor needs around learning. Educators may specialize in programming for specific age groups, from preschool to adult seniors, and may work with audiences ranging from individuals to families to groups. Increasingly, museums (like libraries) are hiring educators trained specifically to work with homeschool groups as well. Museum educators develop programming based on the museum's collections and exhibits (Figure 7.4), evaluate broader learning outcomes, and work with exhibits and curatorial staff to interpret the collections.

Program Developer

In museums with large education departments, in addition to museum educators there may be program developers on staff. A museum program

Figure 7.4 A living history interpreter is one kind of museum educator. K. F. Latham is shown dressed as an early 1830s Amish immigrant at Sauder Village, Archbold, Ohio. Photograph by authors.

developer typically has a degree in museum studies and is a specialist in developing educational programming based on the museum's collection and exhibits.

Audience Evaluator

Some museums have on-staff evaluators who measure the impact of exhibits and other programming on museum audiences, while in other museums this work is contracted out to independent professionals. Evaluators may have a variety of titles, including director, coordinator, and educator. These workers design and carry out evaluations and interpret their findings to the public programming staff. Evaluators may be required to have an understanding of the techniques of audience evaluation, educational theory, environmental design, communication, marketing, and developmental psychology. Evaluator positions usually require a graduate degree in education or museum studies as well as experience in audience evaluation.

Exhibition

Exhibition Developer

Exhibits staff members may have degrees in fine or design arts, often have museum studies training as well, and must be familiar with the use of archival materials as well as traditional design and construction materials. A day in the life of exhibits staff could range from planning and designing a future exhibition to fabricating mounts and building scenes for a current exhibit to cleaning the dust off older exhibits. Although most exhibit staff members are multitalented and able to perform an astoundingly wide variety of tasks related to exhibit design and construction, there are some specialties found in museums, as detailed below. Although larger museums often maintain a full exhibit staff, many smaller institutions use a team approach to exhibit work utilizing staff members from several areas of the museum. Or a museum may contract out exhibit design and fabrication work to private companies or consultants.

Artist

Exhibit artists may have specializations in painting, sculpting, or both. In addition to exhibit design and construction, exhibition artists may make object mounts as well as design, format, and produce labels and other signage in use throughout the museum.

Carpenter

Exhibit carpenters must be adept at framing, specialized building and construction, and finish work. Museum carpenters are called upon to do many complex tasks, from building structures for heavy objects to crafting supports for tiny or fragile objects. Typically, one only finds dedicated carpenters in larger museums.

Designer

Designers are specialists with skills that involve the use of digital and automated design software; an understanding of how to translate complex ideas into visual presentations; and knowledge of how to incorporate fragile, sensitive collection objects into larger storylines. Exhibit designers must have the necessary people skills to work with exhibit fabricators as well as curators, educators, and other content specialists to develop exhibits as part of a team.

Public Relations

Public Relations Officer

Museum public relations personnel must possess exceptional communication skills and have the ability to translate complex ideas into terms understandable to the general public. Most public relations staff members have a degree in journalism, marketing, communications, or advertising.

Security

Security Officer

At one time the main job of the museum security officer was to make sure that the visitors did not touch the exhibits and that nothing was stolen from the collections. However, museum security has become an increasingly complex concern over the last twenty years due to the increase in violent incidents in public places. The contemporary security guard must be trained in public safety assessment, including detection of explosives, dealing with armed intruders, crowd movement and safety, first aid, and museum security systems. The museum security officer has the responsibility to make sure the museum's security, prevention, and detection systems are operating; works with the staff to identify security problems and to safeguard collection storage; screens visitors to protect public safety; works with local, state, and national law enforcement agencies; and hires and trains museum guards. Museum security officers typically have training in criminology or criminal justice, police science, law enforcement, or public safety.

R E A L I T Y   C H E C K

SWAT Team in the Museum

One time, when I was a curator of collections, I was informed that the local SWAT team would be practicing maneuvers in our museum. The labyrinth of dark, underground twists and turns that made up our exhibit halls, I was told, made it perfect for their training needs. However, as most of our exhibits and collections storage were in the basement level where the maneuvers would be held (and at night, to boot), I was understandably very nervous about this. I had thoughts of teams of officers holding large weapons who were unfamiliar with our museum, dashing through the exhibits filled with one-of-a-kind flown spacecraft and other artifacts wearing night-vision goggles. We didn't have a security officer, but we did have a vice president responsible for security, and one of our educators was training to be a police officer, so they assured me all would be safe. In the end, nothing was damaged and, as my VP pointed out to me later, now we had a team of trained officers who knew our site very well and were prepared to handle an emergency for us if necessary. (KFL)

Guard

Museum guards are the side of museum security that is most often visible to the public. Depending on the size of the museum and the content of its collections, a museum may have guards on duty only during public hours, or on a 24/7 basis. Museum guards who work with the public must have good people skills in addition to training in security. In some museums, the guard staff is trained to direct visitors through the museum.

R E A L I T Y   C H E C K

Good Guards Are Worth Their Weight in Gold

I once had a memorable experience at the Toledo Museum of Art (TMA) with one of the guards. It was a moment that helped me realize what a waste it is to simply have guards be silent watchers in the galleries, looking suspiciously at visitors and making them feel uncomfortable. This guard changed my perspective. I walked into one of my favorite galleries, which featured Renaissance period portraits. As I was looking around, getting my bearings, the guard came excitedly up to me, waved me over, and said, "Come here, come here, you have to see this, it's my favorite in the whole museum." He pulled a chair over for me (another great thing at the TMA is the large number of moveable chairs for visitors; see Figure 7.5), positioned it directly in front of a Rembrandt, and gestured for me to sit down. Then he left me, a big smile on his face, to contemplate the painting on my own. (KFL)

Figure 7.5   A chair for visitors to contemplate the art in the Toledo Museum of Art. Photograph by authors.

Maintenance

Facilities Manager

The museum facilities manager, sometimes called the operations manager, has oversight of the physical structure of the museum building, including all electrical, water, security, and heating and cooling systems. Most facilities managers have a background in engineering or technical training in heating, ventilation, and air conditioning (HVAC) systems but must understand the specialized needs of housing museum collections. In older buildings the facilities manager may have to develop a deep understanding of obsolete or long-forgotten building systems that are still in operation. Facilities managers serve as the intermediary between the museum and construction crews when renovations or additions are planned and executed. The facilities manager is usually in charge of custodians and groundskeepers as well as building functions.

Custodian

Custodians do the hard work of cleaning the museum. Though often unappreciated or unnoticed by the other staff members, the role of the custodian is very important to the operation of the building. Custodians usually work under the direction of the facilities manager. While most custodial staff do not need specific backgrounds for the job, it is beneficial to educate them on-site about the special needs of the collections and exhibits. As frontline staff, they can be key players in the care of the museum's unique resources.

Grounds Keeper

The care of the lawn, walkways, and parking areas of the museum is the responsibility of the groundskeepers, under the direction of the facilities manager. The keeping of the grounds isn't entirely for aesthetic purposes. Understanding the landscape's relationship to the building is important to maintaining a dry and safe building and its contents.

REALITY CHECK

Knowing Their Names

The people who perform tasks for the museum, such as cleaning, lawn care, and security, are often taken for granted by museum staff, but they shouldn't be. For example, when we teach collection management, we like to point out that it is the custodians who are most likely to find pest problems in the museum, because their work is usually done before the collections care staff arrive, and cleaning can remove early evidence of pests. Custodians may unintentionally use chemicals in their work that produce vapors that can damage collection objects, so it behooves collection managers to maintain good communication with them. In our courses, we tell students that if they are not on a first-name basis with the custodians, they are not doing their job right. (JES and KFL)

Visitor Services

Visitor Services Coordinator

Some museums have a visitor services coordinator or visitor services director who handles mostly the frontline staff and facilities that aid in providing each visitor with the opportunity to enjoy a heightened museum experience. The way visitor services tasks are divided among staff is highly variable from one museum to another, but it could include anything from the maintenance of visitor reception, orientation, and admission processes down to making sure the restrooms are stocked, coatroom is staffed, and first aid is available for visitors. The person in this position may also be in charge of event planning, the gift shop, and food areas.

Event Planner

Institutions that have spaces that can be rented for public use, such as weddings, birthday parties, or meetings, may have an event planner on staff. The event planner works with the client to arrange catering, music, and crowd management services while protecting the museum's interests. Museum event planners typically have a background in marketing, public relations, or business.

REALITY CHECK

Scratch Your Name into This Important Artifact

Being the museum's resident nay-sayer when I was in charge of collections, I was considered the "don't touch" Grinch. I was not a happy camper when I did a spot check one day on one of our airplanes, an SR-71 Blackbird that was positioned with its nose pointed at an angle near the floor, close to the front entrance, and found graffiti carved into the surface. The way the airplane was positioned, anyone could touch it, and the management did not want signs or barriers around it. I was an 8 a.m. to 5 p.m. staff worker, which meant that I was generally not around after hours or on weekends, and apparently that's when the parties started. We often rented out the space, not in the exhibit halls, but in our entrance. One night I watched the events staff set up tables and noticed something curious. They put several tables right under the nose of the airplane. People would spend an entire evening drinking and eating with that nose hovering right above them. Apparently it was just too enticing to leave blemish free; it didn't occur to guests that this plane was a valuable artifact that had once flown far above the earth. (KFL)

Retail Store Manager

A well-run museum store serves as an adjunct to the exhibits and public programs to enhance the visitor experience. Under the laws that govern nonprofit institutions, the objects offered for sale in the store must reflect the museum's mission and purpose, and in practice they are generally themed to the museum's exhibits or current programs. For these reasons, a museum store manager must demonstrate an understanding of the museum in addition to having a good business and retail sales background.

Research

Curator

As discussed above, in some museums curators conduct research or engage in other scholarly activities. Most research curators do collection-based or collection-related research. Curators who have research responsibilities are more common in large science, art, or history museums than in other sorts of museums. University museum curators are often jointly appointed to an academic department as well as to the museum, so their jobs are a combination of the work done by professors and museum workers.

Librarian

Museum library work is similar to other library work, except that museum libraries are highly specialized, and the librarian must be specialized in the areas of research carried out by curators, exhibit designers, and museum educators. Museum libraries often contain extensive collections of rare books and manuscripts in addition to more traditional library materials. Librarians are usually found only in large museums with intensive research or scholarly missions.

References

Bates, G. W. 1994. *Museum Jobs from A–Z: What They Are, How to Prepare, and Where to Find Them*. Jacksonville, FL: Batax Museum Publishing.

Cato, Pasley S., et al. 1996. *Developing Staff Resources for Managing Collections*. Special Publication No. 4. Martinsville, VA: Virginia Museum of Natural History .

Findlen, Paula. 1994. *Possessing Nature: Museums, Collecting, and Scientific Culture in Early Modern Italy*. Berkeley: University of California Press.

Glaser, Jane R., and Artemis A. Zenetou. 1996. *Museums: A Place to Work. Planning Museum Careers*. New York: Routledge.

Petrie, William F. 1900. "A National Repository for Science and Art." *Royal Society of Arts Journal* 48: 525–533.

Podgorny, Irina. 2012. "Un repositorio nacional para la ciencia y el arte. Traducción, notas y palabras preliminares." Bogotá: Cuadernos de Museología, Universidad Nacional de Colombia.

Roberts, Lisa C. 1997. *From Knowledge to Narrative. Educators and the Changing Museum*. Washington, DC: Smithsonian Books.

Simmons, John E. 2006. "Museum Studies Programs in North America." In *Museum Studies: Perspectives and Innovations*, edited by Stephen L. Williams and Catharine A, Hawks, 113–128. Washington, DC: Society for the Preservation of Natural History Collections.

8

Museum Users

What Is a Museum User?

Museums serve a broad audience. The people who use them have diverse and complex needs, and for this reason, museum professionals need to know something about museum users. A museum user is anyone who uses either the inner or outer museum (see Figure 8.1). Outer museum users include visitors who walk through the door to see exhibits, attend programs, or research collections, or they can be people who use the museum through educational outreach and online resources. Inner museum users include the museum workers themselves, as well as volunteers. This chapter focuses mostly on the point of view of outer museum users, more specifically the users of the museum who do not work or volunteer in it, those who see mostly the public side of museum functioning.

As discussed in Chapter 3, the outer museum involves more than exhibits, gift shops, and restaurants. It's about the transactions between the museum (its contents and programs) and people. Without an audience, a museum is merely a repository or a storehouse. As a system that maintains an irreplaceable and meaningful physical resource, a museum needs a purpose and an audience. To be meaningful, museums need someone—visitors—to make meaning out of this resource. As the definition (see Chapter 1) of a museum states, the museum is a place where visitors interact with ideas and concepts about that resource.

> **Museum:** a system to build and permanently maintain an irreplaceable and meaningful physical resource *and use it to transmit ideas and concepts to the public.*

This chapter explores who museum users are, why and how they use museums, and how museum workers can support museum users' needs, as well as visitor studies, the subfield of museum studies that seeks to understand what motivates museum users.

Figure 8.1   The user in the museum system.

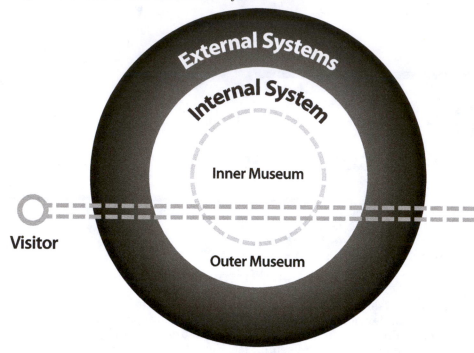

Who Uses Museums?

If it seemed that the inner museum system, the part that is usually behind the scenes, was complex, the outer museum and its users can make the inner museum seem simple and straightforward. After all, the potential audience for museums is *everyone*. Overall, museums are open to all; no one is excluded from having a museum experience, and each visitor brings a unique perspective to the encounter. Even so, this doesn't mean that everyone goes to museums. Barriers can be unconsciously placed or can exist as residual effects of societal norms.

While the range of users runs from a single person to large tour groups, most museum research has focused on specific audiences, such as school groups, families, children, or teens. Certainly studying every possible combination of people who (could) visit museums is next to impossible, but the motivations and needs of individuals and groups who tend to frequent museums most can be investigated. Each group can be defined by some general characteristics that relate to their development and demographic structure. These details cannot be understood alone, but must be evaluated in the context and time in which they occur. In this section, five groups are highlighted: the average visitor, schools and teachers, children and families, young adults, and older adults.

The Average U.S. Museum Visitor

A recent study by Reach Advisors of more than 40,000 museum-going households who visited 103 museums provides a fascinating portrait of museum users in the United States. In art museums, for example, 65 percent of visitors are over age sixty, and of the total number of visitors, 92 percent are white, and 86 percent have at least one college degree. Only 18 percent of art museum visitors are parents of minor children. Science centers, on the other hand, draw a younger audience; 72 percent of their visitors are under age fifty, and 66 percent of them are parents of minor children, most of whom are in elementary school. Of the visitors to science centers, 80 percent have college degrees, and 84 percent are white. The study found that 65 percent of visitors to history museums and historic sites are over age sixty, and 25 percent of them are the parents of minor children, with more than half in middle or high school. Seventy-eight percent of history museum visitors have at least one college degree, and 95 percent are white. Children's museums naturally draw younger visitors, with 89 percent under the age of fifty, and 64 percent under age forty. Children's museum visitors are 89 percent female, and 88 percent of them are parents of young, often preschool, minor children; 81 percent of these visitors have at least one college degree.

Schools and Teachers

Organized groups of schoolchildren have traditionally been a large portion of visitors to museums, but their numbers have been declining over the last decade because of school concerns around preparing students for standardized tests and declining school budgets. Nevertheless, schools and teachers often look to museums to reinforce classroom content. Teachers may use museum resources to provide their students with provocative ideas and different ways to look at an issue. Many museums provide curricula, loan objects, or present guided tours directed to school-aged children. Some museums provide students with opportunities for hands-on experiences with objects through in-house and outreach programs. Others offer professional development for teachers related to their exhibits and ways they might use the museum, making available innovative teaching strategies and new content.

Children and Families

Family audiences make up nearly 40 percent of all museum visitors (Borun 2008). For many families, a trip to the museum is an outing that combines learning, socializing, and entertainment for everyone (Figure 8.2). As a result many museum professionals try to find ways to provide the entire family with positive museum experiences by creating opportunities for families to access museum exhibits and programs and to increase family interaction and connections.

When considering children as visitors, it is important to remember that they use museums in somewhat different ways than adults do. Children can learn new information astoundingly fast, but they learn in different ways over time. Early childhood learning is very concrete, but as children grow older they learn in more abstract ways. The advent of children's museums and science centers emphasized the idea of "hands-on" learning in museum practice.

In 2005 the Institute for Learning Innovation conducted a study at The Children's Museum of Indianapolis on how families used the museum and its learning environments. Because most children visit museums in the company of adults, the study identified four critical aspects to family learning:

Figure 8.2 Pretending to be an astronaut, a fun activity for children at a space museum. Photograph by authors.

- Families need environments that are *developmentally appropriate* for all ages of the family group, from toddlers to grandparents. This means that activities have to accommodate varying abilities and limitations.

- Families seek out playful and social experiences. Everyone wants to see new things and have fun while they are learning. The adults want to engage the children in conversation. Families need an atmosphere in which the parents can read labels aloud to their children and talk about what they are seeing with them.

- Families need to relate their experiences at the museum to their existing knowledge so they can build on that knowledge.

- Family learning involves many different styles of learning.

Young Adults

For many years young adults were a demographic group that was all but ignored in museums, but in recent years museums and other memory institutions are paying more attention to this demographic and their needs and behaviors. Museum visits compete for time with movies, video games, and new technologies, which are much more accessible and more instantly gratifying. Teens tend to like museums with photography, recent history, and explanations of present-day phenomena (technological and scientific), or those that focus on the personal identity of individuals. Teens have a need for personal identification with the stories told in museums and with the methods of narrative and interaction. The more that teens are able to use museums to explore their sense of identity, and in particular the experiences that interest them, the more they will be likely to make museums part of their world.

Older Adults

In their large study of museum visitors, Wilkening and Chung (2009) identified the group of people born between 1927 and 1945 as "The Silent/Mature Generation." This museum audience grew up during the Depression and World War II years. They tend to be prudent with spending in relation to other groups. Most are now retired and increasingly encountering health issues, making physical access important. In the study, the authors found that women and men of this generation are different in their museum behavior. Older women, whom they termed "dream visitors," see museums as valuable, beautiful places of restoration that sustain and engage them as they look for personal, immersive experiences. Older men, also enthusiastic museum-goers, want personal engagement but have more interest in facts and self-guidance, preferring to be given the tools to enjoy their visit and learn something new on their own. Overall, the older adult audience is small, with slightly more women than men, among other reasons possibly due to the frequency of visits with younger family members.

Why and How Do People Use Museums?

This seemingly simple question has no straightforward answer. A single person might use a museum for so many different reasons that it's difficult to tally them up. For any individual person, the reasons can change depending on the day he or she comes, whom the person is with, and how the museum matches personal interests. However, knowing how people decide to use museums is an important part of knowing why they visit in the first place, and research shows that most motivations for using museums can be grouped into a few distinct, overlapping categories, such as to socialize, to reminisce, to play, to relax, and to learn.

People often come to museums with their families or other social groups, and they often come for social reasons. Although visitors may say they come to museums to learn things, more often than not the social agenda takes precedence. To spend quality family time, go on a date, or have something to do with out-of-town guests, or just for a place to hang out with friends, are some of the primary reasons people choose to go to museums.

More personal, individualized experiences are also prevalent. Some visitors see the museum as a place to reminisce, to relax, to find peace, to restore, and to contemplate. Numerous studies over the past several decades have attempted to better understand museum visitors' use and motivations for their visits. Zahava Doering, director of institutional studies at the Smithsonian, argued that rather than communicating information, the "most satisfying exhibitions for visitors will be those that resonate with their experiences and provide new information in ways that confirm and enrich their existing view of the world" (Doering & Pekarik 1997, 47). In other words, people go to museums to make meaning (see Chapter 4). Silverman (1995) stressed that it is important for museum workers to understand that what is at the core of museum experience is *meaning-making*. Referring to this as a paradigm shift, she wanted to fashion a better "fit" between people and museums by infusing notions of meaning-making into museum practice and methods. She also felt that by doing this, museums could validate themselves as a human need in society.

Packer (2008) stated that some experiences in museums go "beyond learning," that the value and benefits of the museum experience impact visitors' ongoing well-being and affect their daily lives in a multitude of ways, such as personal growth, environmental mastery, purpose in life, positive relations, self-acceptance, feeling good as a result of the visit, relaxation, peace and tranquility, and thoughtfulness. Packer's study confirms that satisfying experiences can go beyond traditional learning outcomes.

Furthermore, work done by Falk (2009) suggests that people visit and make meaning from their museum experiences based on identity-related goals and interests and that the reasons people go to museums can be recognized generally through five kinds of identities: explorers, facilitators, experience-seekers, professionals/hobbyists, and rechargers (see Table 8.1.). Explorers are curious persons who love to expand their horizons. Facilitators want their companions to have a good time. Experience seekers want to check off the iconic things on their to-do lists. Professionals/hobbyists have specific, directed goals for their visits, usually related to work or a hobby. Rechargers want a rejuvenating break in a calm setting. According to Falk's study, users take on these identities at different times, but museums may or may not be able to accommodate each identity's associated needs. Falk argues that the way for museums to succeed—in all layers of the museum—is by enhancing and supporting the different identity needs of the users.

How Are User Needs Supported in Museums?

Most people see museums as educational institutions, but what does this mean? Certainly museums are sites of learning, but as discussed in the previous section, they are more than that. Learning is but one of the many things that can happen in a museum. Current research is reviewed next to see how museums can support museum user needs through an understanding of how people learn in museums as well as what their range of needs might be beyond learning.

Supporting Learning in the Museum

Museums are *informal learning environments*, settings within which informal learning opportunities are made available to visitors. Museologists use the terms *informal learning* or *free-choice learning* to describe the "lifelong process whereby every individual acquires attitudes, values, skills, and knowledge from daily experience and the educative influences and resources

Table 8.1   The Five Visitor Identities

Identity	Description
Explorers	• attending museums interests them and appeals to their curiosity • do not have concrete learning goals, but like to know new things • goal is to satisfy a curiosity • highly value learning but are not experts • most likely will be attracted by a new exhibit and the rare items on display • desire to expand their horizons • comprise a large number of visitors • don't want a structured visit • will avoid interpretive tools and guided tours: too restrictive • don't want blockbuster exhibit • will likely read labels
Facilitators	• come because of someone else • personal needs are to make a good experience for others • are price conscious and aware of time • primary motivation is to ensure companion is satisfied
Experience Seekers	• are collecting experiences: checking off a list of things to do • want to do what they are supposed to do in that city or area • want to feel like they've been there, they've done that • want to see the destination, building, or what's iconic on display • may need to see the museum's highlights to feel satisfied • are often tourists but could just be looking for fun things to do on the weekend • are socially motivated and want to have fun with friends or family • are not strongly motivated by the topic • are unlikely to have visited as children • are not likely to be regular museum visitors. • except for the large iconic museums, most museums don't attract large numbers of this category
Professional/Hobbyists	• are the smallest category of visitors but very influential (museum professionals, art and antique collectors, photographers, teachers, artists, historians, etc.) • are often the most critical visitors • come with a goal in mind and are on a mission • are not likely to visit as part of a group • are a micro niche audience
Rechargers	• find the museum a place to get away from it all, to decompress, to reflect, rejuvenate, or just bask in the wonder of a place • see museums as places that afford them the opportunity to avoid the noise of the outside world; museum as respite from the world • visit is almost a spiritual one • tend to avoid crowds or sensations • are fairly self-sufficient • a successful visit will leave them with the feeling that they have gotten away • art museums, botanical gardens, aquariums have a lot of these visitors • are not very concerned with objects; they are just part of the scenery • will rarely be attracted by special exhibits or blockbusters

Based on Falk (2009).

in his or her environment—from family and neighbors, from work and play, from the market place, the library, and the mass media" (Visitor Studies Association 2013). Learning happens differently in museums than it does in formal learning environments such as school classrooms. Informal learning is voluntary and self-directed in such settings, driven by curiosity, discovery, free exploration, and the sharing of experiences with companions. Learning in museums, in its broadest sense, is a by-product of the free interaction of leisure-oriented visitors with exhibitions and their surroundings. Museums, as informal learning environments, offer unlimited potential for communicating social, historic, aesthetic, cultural, and scientific information.

Museum practitioners should be aware that visitors learn in different ways and that communication with audiences should be purposeful and intentional. To sort out the expansive landscape of learning theories and how these affect public programming, Hein (1998) outlined features of learning theories that are useful for analyzing learning in the museum (see Figure 8.3). One aspect of learning theory has to do with the assumptions one makes about the nature of knowledge. Hein represented the wide-ranging ideas about what is learned in a museum as two extremes on a continuum. At one extreme, *knowledge exists outside the learner*, and at the other extreme, *knowledge is created by the learner*. A second aspect of learning theory concerns how learning happens. At one extreme, *learning is considered to be incremental and passive*, while at the other extreme, *the learner actively constructs knowledge*. In Figure 8.3, the juxtaposition of these ideas and how people learn creates four domains—didactic-expository, stimulus-response, discovery, and constructivism—each describing a particular theory of learning that can be applied to museums. Application of a didactic-expository theory means that exhibits and programs should be sequential, with a beginning and an end, and have a clear order. It means that object labels should tell the visitor what is to be learned and be written with a hierarchical arrangement of information, from simple to complex. On the other hand, application of a stimulus-response theory means that information communicated to a visitor should be didactically organized, expository, and have reinforcing components and rewards for response. A discovery-based theory of learning conceptualizes learning as an active process, so that exhibits allow for exploration, will probably not be arranged linearly, and will have a wide range of learning modes. Object labels should ask questions for the visitor to consider. The importance of active participation by the learner

Figure 8.3   Knowledge theories and learning theories. Based on Hein (1998).

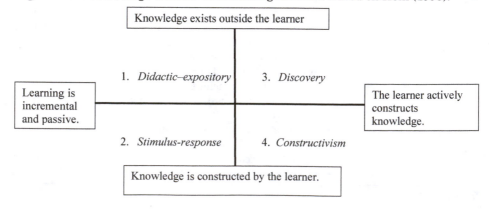

(constructivist learning theory) is gaining currency in museums today. Constructivist exhibits should have many entry points but no specific paths or obvious beginnings or endings, and should include a wide range of learning modes and many points of view. Constructivist exhibits allow learners to connect with objects and ideas through activities and experiences.

Another important and useful framework for understanding learning in informal settings is the Contextual Model of Learning by Falk and Dierking (2000), which conceives of learning as both a process and a product, influenced by three overlapping contexts: personal, physical, and sociocultural (see Figure 8.4). Across these contexts, different factors influence learning in each context.

The personal context refers to the sum total of personal history that a person carries into a learning situation. The key factors that influence learning in the *personal* context are motivation and expectations; prior knowledge, interests, and beliefs; and choice and control. The *sociocultural* context recognizes that people are all socially and culturally situated, which means that they are always influenced by large-scale values, norms, and behaviors that surround them in their daily lives as members of a society. Key factors in this context are within-group sociocultural mediation and facilitated mediation by others. Finally, learning is also acknowledged to take place in a *physical* environment. No matter what people do, they are surrounded by influences such as lighting, space, climate, and physical needs. Advance organizers, design, and reinforcing events and experiences are the

Figure 8.4 The contextual model of learning. Adapted from Falk and Dierking (2000).

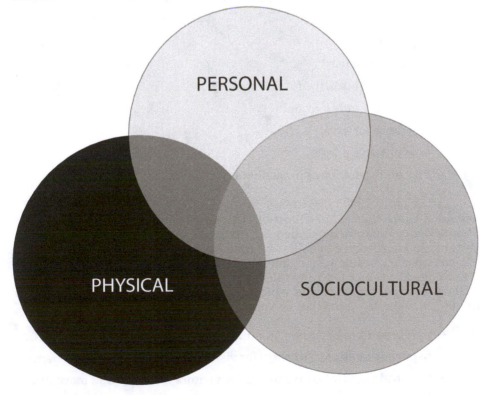

key elements of the physical context. This framework provides a device for museum professionals to organize and understand the complexities of informal learning processes and environments. Overall, the contextual model of learning is a useful tool for thinking about the ways that visitors experience the museum and how they might use the museum to meet various needs.

Universally Designed Museum Experiences

Museum users are a rich and complex group who actively seek out opportunities to learn and connect with museum objects, ideas, and content. To meet the wide range of learning needs for all visitors means that museum workers must take an active approach to creating and designing products and environments that are usable by everyone, to the greatest extent possible, without the need for adaptation or specialized design. Two key ideas, Universal Design and Universal Design for Learning, provide useful frameworks to support all museum users.

Universal Design (UD) originated in architecture to ensure equitable access to spaces and products. Many people think UD is only for people with disabilities, but true UD meets the needs of potential users with a wide variety of characteristics. For example, color choices and contrast of visual materials can provide support for those with low vision as well as those who are color-blind or older adults. Doors that have levers rather than knobs are easier to open for people with limited gripping ability, which could include someone with an armful of materials such as a young child or a person with loss of fine motor function. Universal Design should be considered when developing museum exhibits and programs, because it ensures equitable access by making programs, policies, objects, places, and information more usable for everyone. The key principles in UD (Center for Universal Design 1997) include the following:

- Equitable use
- Flexibility in use
- Simple and intuitive function
- Perceptible information
- Tolerance for error
- Low physical effort
- Size and space for approach and use

In the early 1990s the Center for Applied Special Technology (CAST) extended UD to the field of education. Universal Design for Learning (UDL) provides a framework for designing curricula to enable all individuals to better gain knowledge and skills and take an interest in learning. It is a philosophy that frames how learning opportunities are designed, grounded in knowledge about how learning takes place (Hitchcock and Stahl 2003). The UDL framework proposes that educators strive for three kinds of flexibility related to brain networks that are activated in learning:

- to represent information in multiple formats and media;
- to provide multiple pathways for visitors' actions and expressions; and
- to provide multiple ways to engage visitors' interests and motivation.

Table 8.2   Components of a Universally Designed Learning Experience

Multiple means of representation	Learners have a variety of ways to acquire information and knowledge.
Multiple means of expression	Learners have alternative means for demonstrating what they know.
Multiple means of engagement	Learners' interests are piqued; they are appropriately challenged and motivated to learn.

When planning museum programming that is accessible and inclusive, useful points of reference are the principles created for the Universal Design for Learning Environments, developed by CAST (see Table 8.2).

In the museum setting, components of a universally designed learning experience are multilayered and multifaceted. *Multiple means of representation* might mean providing many examples to illustrate a theme, highlighting important information, presenting content using different media and formats, and building or activating background knowledge. Providing *multiple means of expression* can be accomplished by modeling skills in a variety of ways, presenting opportunities through scaffolding (i.e., providing supportive resources upon which learners can build their confidence and abilities), giving corrective feedback, and allowing alternatives for users to demonstrate learning (see Figure 8.5). *Multiple means of engagement* might

Figure 8.5   Visitors creating their own sculptures in Imagine the Possibilities at the Columbus Museum of Art, Ohio. Photo by CMA.

Figure 8.6   Encountering an object with touch. Photograph by the authors.

include providing visitor input opportunities and showing how they will shape future learning endeavors or allowing visitors to represent or engage in the material and content of programs (see Figure 8.6).

How Do We Know What Users Like?

To understand museum user needs, likes, and dislikes, it is necessary to ask the users themselves. Asking involves a range of activities to investigate ways that visitors use museums, from simply watching them as they experience an exhibit or program; to timing their stops at displays or objects; to conducting surveys (textual or oral), focus groups, and interviews. Visitor evaluation should be an integral part of the museum process, just as collecting objects, developing exhibits, and balancing the budget are. Finding out what users think about programs across all stages of development can help museum workers make crucial decisions about investing resources and can open up a path of communication that involves the transfer of ideas to the public and back.

Visitor Studies

Visitor studies refers to the interdisciplinary study of human experiences within informal learning environments and utilizes systematic collection and analysis of information to inform decisions about exhibits and programs. In general, visitor studies can be divided into evaluation (i.e., targeted specific feedback about a program or exhibit) and audience research (which includes broad aspects of visitor experience), but there is a lot of overlap between these categories. It is becoming much more common for museums to pay attention to their visitors and invest the resources necessary to evaluate the effectiveness of their exhibitions before, during, and after installation. Such attention can increase the learning potential and the enjoyment of museum visits.

Visitor evaluations can take many forms; there is no single perspective or approach that is considered the standard. Methods include live or online surveys, timing and tracking, observation, interviews, and other techniques. The types of evaluation range from prototyping a program or exhibit (front-end evaluation) to testing it while in progress (formative evaluation) to finding out after it's done just how it was received (summative evaluation). Evaluation data are always collected deliberately and systematically. Visitors are studied under many circumstances: in exhibit settings, during school visits, or during interactions between individual visitors and objects.

Audience research is a part of visitor studies: the study of the interactions between visitors and museums and the study of the characteristics, interests, and motivations of different audience segments. It involves the systematic gathering of information (descriptive, psychological, and contextual) about visitors or audiences. Audience research provides museums with a better understanding of the needs and expectations of visitors, can promote visitor engagement, and is useful to make the case to funders and inform interpretation and programming.

Because all audience research should be intentional, the Museums Association (2013) in the United Kingdom suggests that several questions be asked before conducting audience research:

- What do you want to find out?
- Why do you want to find this out?
- What will be done with the information?
- How are you going to find this out?
- Who are you finding this out from?
- How are you going to tell them?
- How much time, staff, and money will be needed?

- What kind of data do you want to collect (quantitative, qualitative, or a mixture)?

- Will you conduct it in-house or hire a consultant?

For many years, evaluation of and research on visitor experiences were considered an extra, nonessential component of museum work, something that only the larger museums could afford. However, understanding the visitor is now recognized as an essential part of museum planning and operation. Communication in two directions—from museum to visitor and from visitor to museum—is preferred. This is where the definition of museum used in this book has one shortcoming; it implies that the experience is unidirectional, that museums *give* or transmit ideas and concepts *to* visitors. In practice visitors also bring important things to the encounter. As discussed in Chapter 4, this scenario is more of a back and forth transaction rather than simply a one-directional movement of ideas. The document-centered museum is the intersection of people and objects and the flow of thoughts, ideas, and experiences that move in all directions; this involves feedback and implementation of results.

References

Art Beyond Sight. n.d. http://www.artbeyondsight.org/handbook/dat-accessible-museum .shtml.

Borun, Minda. 2008. "Why Family Learning in Museums?" *Exhibitionist* (Spring): 6–9.

Burgstahler, Sheryl. 2007. "Universal Design: Principles, Process, and Applications. http://www.washington.edu/doit/.

Center for Universal Design. 1997. "The Principles of Universal Design." http://www .ncsu.edu/www/ncsu/design/sod5/cud/about_ud/udprinciplestext.htm.

Doering, Zahava D., and Andrew J. Pekarik. 1997. "Visitors to the Smithsonian Institution: Some Observations." *Visitor Studies* 9, no. 1: 40–50.

Falk, John H. 2009. *Identity and the Museum Visitor Experience*. Walnut Creek, CA: Left Coast Press.

Falk, John H., and Lynn D. Dierking. 2000. *Learning from Museums: Visitor Experiences and the Making of Meaning*. Walnut Creek, CA: Altamira Press.

Falk, John H., and Martin Storksdieck. 2005. "Using the Contextual Model of Learning to Understand Visitor Learning from a Science Center Exhibition." *Science Education* 89, no. 5: 744–778.

Hein, George F. 1998. *Learning in the Museum*. New York: Routledge.

Hitchcock, C., and S. Stahl. 2003. "Assistive Technology, Universal Design, Universal Design for Learning: Improved Learning Opportunities." *Journal of Special Education Technology* 18, no. 4: 45–52.

Jewitt, Carey, ed. 2009. *The Routledge Handbook of Multimodal Analysis*. London: Routledge.

Joy, Annika. 2012. "Embedding Audience Research." http://www.museumsassociation .org/museum-practice/audience-research/15082012-embedding-audience -research.

Museums Association. 2013. "A Basic Guide to Audience Research. http://www .museumsassociation.org/museum-practice/audience-research/15082012 -guide-to-audience-research (accessed September 1, 2013).

Packer, Jan. 2008. "Beyond Learning: Exploring Visitor's Perceptions of the Value and Benefits of Museum Experiences." *Curator* 51, no. 1: 33–54.

Perry, Deborah, Lisa Roberts, Kris Morrissey, and Lois Silverman. 1996. "Listening Outside and Within." *The Journal of Museum Education* 21, no. 3: 26–27.

Reach Advisors. 2010. "Museum Audience Insight." http://reachadvisors.typepad.com.

Silverman, Lois H. 1995. "Visitor Meaning-Making in Museums for a New Age." *Curator* 38, no. 3: 161–170.

Stephens, Simon. 2012. "A Basic Guide to Audience Research." *Museum Practice* (August).   http://www.museumsassociation.org/museum-practice/audience-research/15082012-guide-to-audience-research.

Visitor Studies Association. 2013. "Glossary." http://visitorstudies.org/resources/professional-development/glossary (accessed January 1, 2014).

Wilkening, Susie, and James Chung. 2009. *Life Stages of the Museum Visitor: Building Engagement Over a Lifetime*. Washington, DC: American Alliance of Museum Press.

Section Five
Where

9

Contemporary Museums Around the World

Museums in the Contemporary World

Although museums have their origins in Western Europe, they can now be found in almost every country in the world. As discussed in Chapter 2, it is important to note that there were traditions of collecting in many parts of the world long before there were museums.

While there is no exact count of contemporary museums worldwide or even country-by-country, the 19th edition of the reference book *Museums of the World* (2012) lists more than 55,000 museums divided into 22 categories in 202 countries, and 500 professional museum associations in 132 countries. Museums vary quite a bit from country to country in how and what they collect, how they interpret their collections, their funding and governing structures, and what they sell in their gift shops. One of the most fundamental differences between museums in the United States and those in other countries is that the latter are largely government funded or at least heavily government subsidized and government controlled; therefore, most museum workers are government employees. Few other countries have the equivalent of the nonprofit sector provided for by U.S. tax law.

Internationally, the United Nations Educational, Scientific and Cultural Organization (UNESCO), the International Council of Museums (ICOM), the International Council of Monuments and Sites (ICOMOS), and the International Center for the Preservation of Cultural Property (ICCROM) are the largest organizations serving museums. These organizations work at the international level, providing assistance to museums with the formulation of policies and codes of ethics; providing models for museum structure and professional training; and producing manuals to guide registration, exhibition, and other museum operations and practices. In addition, all four organizations play some role in trying to foster cross-border cooperation among museums. The ICOM Information Center (located in Paris, France) is the largest repository of museum information in the world.

Although museums were established in some non-European countries in the early nineteenth century, it was the 1970 Convention on the Means of Prohibiting and Preventing the Illicit Import, Export and Transfer of

Ownership of Cultural Property, commonly known as the UNESCO Convention, that set the tone for the sorts of museums that populate the world today. Under the terms of the UNESCO Convention, protected objects of cultural property are subject to seizure if they are illegally exported from their country of origin and imported into another signatory country. The UNESCO Convention has been a significant factor in reducing the illicit international trade in cultural patrimony, which in turn has fostered the growth of national museums by keeping cultural resources within their countries of origin. Unfortunately, despite this and other international agreements, much cultural property is still at risk due to the thriving black market in such objects. In addition to protecting cultural patrimony, the UNESCO Convention has established standards that have impacted the development of museums in many countries. These standards include defining archaeological material as objects of cultural significance that are at least 250 years old, and defining objects of ethnographic interest as products of tribal or nonindustrial societies that are important to the cultural heritage of a people because of their distinctive characteristics, rarity, or relevance to the history of the people. Establishing these definitions has helped museums around the world communicate more clearly with one another and helped reduce the illegal trade in cultural heritage artifacts. On a broad scale, the UNESCO Convention helped establish the concept of museums as trusted protectors and preservers of community heritage, national heritage, cultural objects, and traditions, and has reinforced the obligation of museums to properly manage and present the collections they hold.

The Effects of Globalization

Global Diversity

Some museums have well-established international reputations and have become so well known that people recognize their names even if they have never visited them. Examples include the British Museum in London, the Louvre in Paris, the Prado in Madrid, the Hermitage in St. Petersburg, and Cairo's Egyptian Museum. Although these are all certainly fine museums, they all reflect the traditional Western European ideal of the museum. It is the many lesser-known or practically unknown museums that often show a particular national or cultural influence in what they collect and how their collections are interpreted, as these museums mainly serve local, community audiences. For example, consider the Struwwelpeter Museum, the Thai Folk Songs Museum, or the Museo Histórico de la Policia Nacional. Frankfurt, Germany, hosts the Struwwelpeter Museum, dedicated to a series of children's books written by Heinrich Hoffman in the late 1800s. Although the Struwwelpeter stories strike most American readers as inappropriate for children, they are beloved cultural icons in Germany. The Thai Folk Songs Museum in Bangkok exhibits personal effects of significant Thai folk musicians and maintains archives of printed and recorded folk songs. The Museo Histórico de la Policia Nacional can be found in Bogotá, Colombia; among its exhibits are a motorcycle once owned by drug kingpin Pablo Escobar and a bloody tile from the rooftop in Medellin where Escobar was killed. In each of these examples, the museum collections are focused on culturally specific materials unique to the countries they are found in. In the past, most smaller museums such as these were largely unknown except to locals or tourists, but globalization has changed this situation; now any museum with access to the Internet can have a global presence.

Viva la Revolución

In El Salvador a number of years ago, I had the opportunity to see what was simultaneously one of the worst museums and one of the best museums I have ever seen, all in the same place. I was working in Morazán province, on the border with Honduras, helping to train ex-guerilla fighters as ecotourism guides. One long, hot afternoon, one of the trainees suggested that we walk to Perquín and take a look at the Museo de la Revolución (Museum of the Revolution). Perquín is a tiny little town in the mountains that was the headquarters of the Frente Farabundo Martí de Liberación Nacional (FMLN) during the civil war in El Salvador that raged from 1980 until 1992. The museum is housed in an old school building. It was not a very good museum, in that the exhibits were crude, the labels were inadequate, and the conservation of the artifacts was a disaster. However, it was one of the best museums I have ever seen because it told the story of Perquín the way the people of the community had chosen to tell it, with their own interpretation of the objects that they themselves had collected. The exhibits began with the prehistory of Perquín, but focused on the civil war. The artifacts included a hodgepodge collection of rusty firearms, parts of U.S.-made planes and helicopters that were shot down, and the bombed out broadcast studio of Radio Venceremos. The story that the museum presented was vivid, and the people of Perquín were proud that their museum told their story. And of course, like any good museum, the Museo de la Revolución has both a gift shop and a Web site. (JES)

Global Reach

Beginning in the 1980s, increasing globalization reduced the isolation of many geographic regions and increased the dispersal of information across international borders. With the growth of international reach through the Internet, more knowledge has been made available in more areas of the world, which has profoundly affected the development of museums and other cultural institutions. This shift has also helped museums attract new audiences and increase professionalization globally. Museums that were once isolated in hard to reach, remote geographical areas can now serve and be served by an international audience through digitization of their collections, virtual exhibits, and electronic publication. With an Internet presence, small and specific museums can share their content and collections with a larger audience. This has led to a greater diversity of museums and museological approaches worldwide. Staff in many non-Western museums no longer copy traditional Western museum practices, but instead adapt museum functions to their culture and environment, often based on standards published by ICOM. By making information about museology and museography available online, more knowledge about concepts and practices can be shared across cultures, which has extended the influence of ICOM as an international museum organization. ICOM routinely publishes manuals and other museum publications in English, French, Spanish, and sometimes other languages and makes them available free via its Web site. In addition, thanks to the availability of its publications on the Internet, many smaller organizations, such as the Instituto Liderazgo en Museos (Institute for Museum Leadership, ILM) in Mexico and the South African Museums Association (SAMA), also have influence beyond the bounds of the geographic areas they officially serve. The end result is that different geographic regions have developed their own museological processes and directions (Dickey et al. 2013).

Despite the advantages that globalization presents, almost all of the funding for international cooperation in projects among museums has been concentrated on the exchange of exhibits, or more commonly, bringing cultural heritage from other areas to Western Europe, the United States, and Canada for exhibition. Little funding has been available for projects that deal with international cooperation in collecting or collections care and management, or with conservation, aside from some admirable programs offered by the Getty Conservation Institute.

Protecting Cultural Patrimony

The growing awareness of the need to protect cultural patrimony from theft and destruction, through the actions of UNESCO and other organizations, has been a major factor in the creation of many national museums worldwide.

In some instances, museums have provided a means for cultural and tribal groups to control the interpretation and presentation of their culture, such as the Auckland Museum in New Zealand and its relationship with the native Maori community. In many parts of the world, including the United States, indigenous curation practices are being implemented that are interwoven with contemporary standards for the care of collections, in recognition of the cultural importance of objects in the collections. For example, in some museums in the United States, Native American representatives conduct ritual cleansing of artifacts with sage smoke as part of the spiritual care for sacred objects, male and female objects may be separated in storage and on exhibition, and the handling of some objects may be tightly restricted. In Thailand, representations of the Buddha in collections are stored and exhibited at eye level or above to demonstrate respect for Buddhist beliefs.

National Identity

Some international museums are the products of emerging nationalist movements, helping to define national identity, such as the national system of museums in Nigeria, which has played an important role in defining the culture of postrevolution Nigeria. The Museum of Anthropology in Mexico City helped weave together Mexico's prehistoric past with its war for independence (1810–1821) to provide a new interpretation of what it meant to be Mexican. Some colonial museums, originally established by Western Europeans, have been repurposed to tell a more balanced view of history and help define a postindependence national identity. Many museums in post-apartheid South Africa began to change in the late 1990s to present new interpretations of native cultures and South African history (Witz 2006). Several new museums have been established as well, including the Nelson Mandela National Museum at Mandela's birthplace in Qunu; the Robben Island Museum in Cape Town, which interprets the prison where several key anti-apartheid leaders were held; the Apartheid Museum in Johannesburg; and the Lwandle Migrant Labour Museum in Lwandle. The Lwandle museum is a community history museum devoted to the migrant labor workforce that served the fruit and canning industry under apartheid. The Cape Coast Castle Museum in Ghana worked with international partners to develop and install an exhibit about slavery called "Crossroads of People, Crossroads of Trade," which opened in 1994. After working through many controversies over how the story should be told, the final exhibit presented 500 years of Ghanaian history and the slave trade (Kreamer 2006).

The evolution of many Asian museums shows patterns of development that differ from those in other non-Western regions. Although European missionaries to China introduced the European museum concept in the late nineteenth century, the first true national Chinese museum was not established until 1905 (the Nantong Museum, Beijing). During the first half of the twentieth century, Chinese museums primarily reflected the museological values of Western Europe, but beginning in the 1950s they were heavily influenced by Soviet museology. By the 1980s Chinese museology was developing museums that reflected Chinese cultural and national values, with many museums, including ecomuseums, being established. Between the early 1980s and the late 1990s the number of museums in China doubled, from about 1,000 to nearly 2,000. Today there are an estimated 3,589 museums in China, all but 535 of which are government owned. By contrast, most museums and historic sites in Vietnam reflect the older traditional Western museum model, while telling a story of perseverance against adversity in pursuit of national unity aimed primarily at foreign tourists rather than national citizens. The National Museum of Cambodia, established as the Albert Sarraut Museum in 1917 under the French administration, began as a museum of largely Western art exhibiting copies of famous Western paintings. The museum began to flourish as tourists flocked to Cambodia from the 1920s until independence in 1953. The museum's collections now include national art, historic objects, and prehistoric artifacts (Muan 2006).

Museums in Thailand vary from traditional, Western-style national museums and science museums to open-air historic and archaeological parks. A publication available in Thailand for visitors, for example, lists one hundred museums in Bangkok and its vicinity, ranging from the major national museums and historic sites to museums devoted to sewing machines, bicycles, Siamese cats, and antique clocks (Pulsap 2004).

In most Latin American countries, museums were established during the colonial period prior to independence; after independence, these museums often became the new national museums, along with other new museums and historic sites that were preserved as tangible heritage, often playing a role in the establishment of national identity and helping define a national culture. Nevertheless, for nearly a hundred years most Latin American museums still followed the old colonial model of presenting history as a series of heroic acts carried out by great leaders. The Museo del Hombre Dominicano (Museum of Dominican Man) in the Dominican Republic was founded in 1972 by the national government, based on contemporary museums in the United States in both organization and architecture. For decades the museum's exhibits focused almost exclusively on the preconquest Taino culture of the island of Hispaniola. In the mid-2000s the museum staff began to incorporate the island's African cultural influences into the museum exhibits, enabling the museum for the first time to reflect the culture of the majority of the Dominican Republic's population.

Beginning in the 1980s Latin American museology became much more inclusive, moving beyond the social values established by the dominant elite class to reinterpret the past and present history and culture from many points of view, particularly from indigenous and working-class perspectives. Today many museums in Latin America function as agents of social change, emphasizing their educational and informational role in the community, and make efforts to attract a diverse audience (e.g., most of the museums in Bogotá, Colombia, are open for free one Sunday each month by order of the city government). In areas of Latin America where indigenous languages are still widely used, some museums have signage or audio interpretation in the appropriate indigenous language in addition to Spanish or Portuguese. As discussed below, Latin American countries have also shown a strong interest in ecomuseums and children's museums.

Museums in Africa and the Middle East are relatively new, many holding great world treasures, such as those found in the Museum of Egyptian Antiquities in Cairo. The first museum in Morocco, the Dar Batha Museum in Fez, was opened in 1915 under the colonial administration of the French. Although there are now more than thirty museums in the country, 75 percent of Moroccans have never been to a museum, largely because most of the museums still reflect colonial museological ideals such as interpreting national history from the point of view of the former colonial power or presenting ethnic groups as if they were frozen in the historic past. Recently the Ben M'sik Community Museum in Morocco has broken new ground by interpreting its local community's history and culture. In the countries of the Arabian Gulf area the oldest museum, the Qatar National Museum, dates only to 1975; the recent growth of museums in the region reflects a new societal awareness of the role of cultural patrimony in establishing national identity. Israel now has nearly 200 museums; in 1984 national museum regulations were enacted that established standards for museum operations and the training of museum personnel. One of the newest museums in the Middle East is the Women's Museum of the United Arab Emirates in Dubai, also the first in the region that focuses on art by women and women's rights.

Ecomuseums: An Emerging Global Trend?

The newest category of international museums is the ecomuseum, which appeared in the 1960s and 1970s (see Chapter 5). Ecomuseums are purposely difficult to define, but were developed in reaction to natural history museums, which were seen as enclosing nature within cabinets and buildings. In an ecomuseum, the outside environment is part of the museum collection. The idea of the ecomuseum originated with the *heimatmuseums* (homeland museums) of nineteenth-century Germany, the *skänsen* (open air museums) of Sweden, and the folk museums of Britain. The name *ecomuseum* was coined by two French museologists, Hugues de Varine and Georges Henri Rivière, from the Greek word *oikos*, meaning house, household, or family.

The basic idea behind the ecomuseum is to preserve heritage in situ, as a cultural landscape, so the museum exists in a continuous process of evolution. Museal institutions that call themselves ecomuseums range from villages in which the inhabitants and the village itself constitute the museum, to re-creations of past cultures and living groups. The Ceumannan-Staffin Ecomuseum, for example, is comprised of thirteen different sites on the Isle of Skye in Scotland and advertises itself as a museum without walls that tells the story of the people and the environment of the island. The Ecomuseum Bergslagen, founded in 1986 in Ludvika, Sweden, interprets an area of central Sweden ranging from the medieval town Norberg to mines, homesteads, iron works, and canals. The Alsace Ecomuseum in Ungersheim, France, consists of seventy-three Alsatian village buildings that were relocated to the site. The Tang'an Dong Ethnic Ecomuseum in Zhaoxing, China, includes

170 households and more than 800 residents. The museum was cofounded with help from the Norwegian government and calls itself a people-centered living museum. The Dong community that lives in the ecomuseum practices traditional lifestyles of farming and weaving.

The most recent growth in ecomuseums has been seen in Asia—in Cambodia, China, Japan, Thailand, and Vietnam—and in Europe in Scandinavia, the Czech Republic, Poland, Portugal, and Turkey. The first ecomuseum meeting was held in Rio de Janeiro, Brazil, in 1992, and the first international conference on ecomuseums and community museums was held in Portugal in 2012.

Summary

Many museums around the world look nothing like museums in the United States. World museums have taken many forms as the traditional European museum model has evolved and been adapted to fit the needs of a diverse array of cultures. As a result, there is a stunning variety of museal institutions in the world, many of which blur the lines of traditional categories of museums. A good example of such a museum is the Parque Histórico de Guayaquil (Historic Park of Guayaquil) in Ecuador. The museum is on a twenty-acre site on the banks of the Río Duale across the river from Ecuador's largest city, Guayaquil, which has two million inhabitants. The park interprets the Province of Guayaquil in the late nineteenth and early twentieth centuries, as it was undergoing significant changes following a massive fire in Guayaquil in 1896. The historic park was established by the Central Bank of Ecuador in 1997; upon the completion of the park in 2012, it was turned over to La Empresa Pública de Parques Naturales y Espacios Públicos (Public Agency for Natural Parks and Public Spaces), an agency of the provincial government. Part of the park looks at first glance like a botanical garden and a zoo. The botanical garden is devoted to native plants of the area and sells them to visitors to encourage the preservation of the natural flora of the region. What looks like a zoo is called the Zona de Vida Silvestre (Wildlife Zone) and includes both culturally important animals of the region and several threatened and endangered species, including the American crocodile, which is endangered, and the white-tailed deer, once an important source of protein in the region. The animals are housed in natural habitats rather than traditional zoo cages. Two large areas of re-created mangroves are included, because mangrove habitats were once a vitally important ecosystem along the coast of Ecuador, but most have been destroyed to make shrimp farms. The Zona Tradiciones (Zone of Traditions; see Figure 9.1) interprets the rural *montuvio* culture (*montuvio* refers to people of mixed Spanish, Native American, and African descent who traditionally lived as agriculturalists, hunters, and trappers in coastal Ecuador). The Zona Tradiciones includes a plantation with an old hacienda house, plantings of traditional food crops, farm animals, and a peasant's house with thatch roof. Costumed reenactors interpret the traditional inhabitants of the plantations. Several historic wooden buildings that once stood on the streets of Guayaquil were relocated to the park to create the Zona Urbano Arquitectonica (Urban Architectural Zone), depicting Guayaquil as it was in 1900. The buildings serve as shops for local artisans and craftspeople, who demonstrate the crafts of the era and sell what they produce. It is hard to categorize the Parque Histórico de Guayaquil.

Figure 9.1   Rural house re-created in the Zona Tradiciones of the Parque Histórico de Guayaquil (Ecuador). Photograph by the authors.

Is it a zoo, a botanical garden, an open-air history museum like Colonial Williamsburg, or an ecomuseum? It is all of these, and at the same time, it is none of them; it is a museal institution that has been created to serve its community, a long way from the traditional European museum in form, but very similar in function.

References

Camin, Giulia. 2007. *Los Grandes Museos del Mundo*. Mexico City: Numen.

Cummins, Alissandra. 2006. "Caribbean Museums—Development and Cultural Identity." *ICOM Study Series* 12: 14–17.

Davis, Peter. 1999. *Ecomuseums: A Sense of Place*. London: Leicester University Press.

Dickey, Jennifer W., et al. 2013. *Museums in a Global Context: National Identity, International Understanding*. Washington, DC: The AAM Press.

Glaser, Jane R., and Artemis A. Zenetou. 1996. *Museums: A Place to Work; Planning Museum Careers*. New York: Routledge.

ICCROM. n.d. International Center for the Preservation of Cultural Property. http://www.iccrom.org.

ICOM. n.d. International Council of Museums. http://icom.museum.

ICOMOS. n.d. International Council of Monuments and Sites. http://www.icomos.org/en.

ILM. n.d. Instituto Liderazgo en Museos. http://www.ilmuseos.org.

Kaplan, Flora E. S., ed. 1994. *Museums and the Making of "Ourselves": The Role of Objects in National Identity*. London: Leicester University Press.

Karp, Ivan, et al., eds. 2006. *Museum Frictions: Public Cultures/Global Transformations*. Durham, NC: Duke University Press.

Kreamer, Christine M. 2006. "Shared Heritage, Contested Terrain: Cultural Nego-
tiations and Ghana's Cape Coast Castle Museum Exhibition, 'Crossroads of
People, Crossroads of Trade'," in *Museum Frictions: Public Cultures/Global
Transformations*, edited by Ivan Karp et al., 435–465. Durham, NC: Duke University Press.

Maggi, M., and V. Falletti. 2000. *Ecomuseums in Europe: What They Are and What
They Can Be*. Working Paper no. 137. Torino: Instituto Richerche Economico-
Sociali del Piemonte.

Muan, Ingrid. 2006. "Musings on Museums from Phnom Phen," in *Museum Frictions:
Public Cultures/Global Transformations*, edited by Ivan Karp and others, 257–
285. Durham, NC: Duke University Press.

Museo de la Revolución. n.d. http://perquinelcorazondemorazan.es.tl/museo-de-la
-revoluci%F3n.htm.

Museums of the World. 2012. Munich: De Gruyter Saur.

Pulsap, Sanjai, ed. 2004. *100 Museums in Bangkok and Its Vicinity: The Whole World
Within Reach*. Bangkok: Plan Readers Publisher.

Rico Manrard, L. F. 2001. "Tradition and Modernity in Archaeological and Historical
Museums in Latin America." *ICOM Study Series* 9: 21–22.

Su, D. 2001. "Museology and Cultural Heritage Policies in China." *ICOM Study Series* 9: 13–14.

UNESCO. n.d. United Nations Educational, Scientific and Cultural Organization.
http://en.unesco.org.

Witz, Leslie. 2006. "Transforming Museums on Postapartheid's Tourist Routes," in
Museum Frictions: Public Cultures/Global Transformations, edited by Ivan
Karp and others, 107–134. Durham, NC: Duke University Press.

Zenetou, Artemis A. 1996. "Museums Around the World," in *Museums: A Place to
Work; Planning Museum Careers*, edited by Jane R. Glasser and Artemis A.
Zenetou, 206–226. New York: Routledge.

Section Six
Why

10

The Future of Museums

Why Museums?

Thus far, this book has presented a dynamic view of museums as constantly changing, adaptable institutions; explored the idea that museums are about people and objects and the systems in which they encounter each other; and shown how the document-centered museum brings people and objects together to enable visitors who encounter them to create meaning and understanding for themselves. Contemporary museums are emergent institutions formed by the ever-changing interactions between people and objects (J. Bell 2012). But deeper questions remain: Why *do* museums exist? Why are they needed? What is their future?

Gosden, Larson, and Petch (2007), in their ethnography of the Pitt Rivers Museum in Oxford, England, see museums as relational entities, where people not only collect objects but "objects collect people," revealing that musealized objects begin a chain of new interactions that would not have occurred had they not been presented in the context of a museum. The museum is a system that builds and permanently maintains irreplaceable and meaningful physical resources—documents—and also brings together people whose trajectories only intersect *because* of the collection. Visitors, researchers, workers, collectors, and the other people associated with the object before and after it enters the museum are what make museums relational entities.

Museums today are understood to be dynamic and constantly evolving institutions in society. At the same time, museums are self-aware. This means that museum professionals are paying attention to what goes on around them and know that in order for museums to survive, they must understand not only their users, but also the people who *do not* use museums. Breaking down the walls between the inner and outer museum, and between the internal system (the museum itself) and external systems (the outside world), is becoming increasingly important and common.

In this context, museum staff are realizing the impact their institutions have on society. What museums do—particularly through programs and exhibits—makes statements, sometimes controversial, sometimes not. The ideas, statements, and objects that museum workers choose and the way they present them is a process of selection that always leaves something out because there is no way to include everything. This means that museum staff take epistemological positions in every activity they perform. Even the less publicly visible selection of objects for the collection (registration and collection management) involves making choices about what counts and what doesn't for future generations. Hooper-Greenhill argues that "museums have the opportunity to push at existing borders, to change current relationships, to manipulate and break down old orthodoxies, to enable a broader, more inclusive approach to a more inclusive society" (2000, 573), and this is becoming a major part of what museums do.

This chapter addresses the future and purpose(s) of museums. It is important to know where museums are today, but it is even more important that the people who work in them (and those who hope to work in them) keep an eye on future trends and changes that will likely shape museums of the future.

What Is the Future of Museums?

Healthy museums never seem to stand still, but are always in the process of changing and redefining themselves. With the fast pace of change and innovation in society and the heavy reliance on current and developing technologies, museum staff must work hard to keep up with changes and be innovators in a large, complex, and rapidly evolving world. The following four areas are explored here; all are important for today's museums and will affect the future of the museum in society:

- the virtual and the real,
- sustainability and funding,
- shifting demographics and museum audiences, and
- globalization and localization.

These are not the only issues of concern for museums in the future, but they get at the heart of a fundamental question: Will museums remain relevant?

The Virtual and the Real

In the previous chapters, issues surrounding physical objects and the digitally ubiquitous world were contemplated. Recent trends are profoundly shifting an entire generation's knowledge structures as children are immersed in a world of virtual things and are not growing up in the same world as their parents or grandparents did.

It is important to reiterate that one aspect of the issue of virtuality centers around being in the presence of a physical collection *versus* ease of access to information, as was addressed in the study about users of historical library material by Duff and Cherry (2000), discussed in Chapter 1. Another recent study investigated museum visitors' experiences with physical museum objects by interviewing twenty-one museum visitors ranging in age from twenty to eighty years of age, and from a range of museum types: history, art, natural history, living history, and science centers (Latham n.d.). The participants were asked what "the real thing" in the museum meant to them. Most respondents replied that the physical, original object held something special that replicas, digital versions, and other media versions did not. There is something ineffable, something unique, about being in the presence of an actual object from another time or place. This is supported by other research, such as that done by Reach Advisors in a 2010 survey of museum visitors. When respondents were asked about meaningful museum experiences (defined as how adults engage emotionally and intellectually with museum content), the themes that emerged centered around connections to content, information learned, and hands-on experiences. However, the most significant theme mentioned was *original objects*. Respondents were twice as likely to mention an original object as they were to mention information learned, and the original object was mentioned more than four times as often as hands-on experiences.

Some commentators have suggested that the future of the physical museum is threatened by the rise of virtual museums; however, such speculations ignore the significance of the object's role in museums and in people's lives overall. Virtual exhibits and digital collections have proven to be wonderful resources that enhance physical museums and serve as a means to reach wider audiences (see figure 10.1). However, even though digitization makes more collections and archives accessible, studies show that a museum's presence on the Web ultimately attracts more visitors to the physical museum (Marty 2007), rather than serving as an alternative to the physical museum. People still like to see "the real thing," the physical object. It is important to step back, take a more expansive view, and remember that human beings routinely use objects to navigate their way through the world (MacGregor 2010; Hodder, 2012); it cannot be taken for granted that humans still exist in a world surrounded by physical objects.

Figure 10.1   A visitor rolls digital clay at the Cleveland Museum of Art's Gallery One. Photograph by authors.

The Sustainable Museum and Funding

If museums are going to continue to be the repositories of physical collections and sites for meaning-making, some serious financial issues must be addressed. Many people think that being nonprofit means that museums are supported by government funds, but museums in the United States receive less than a quarter of their funding from government sources (F. Bell 2012). Financial resources for museums from government sources have declined from 39.2 percent to just 24.4 percent of museum funding since 1989. Earned income, including admission charges, rental of space, and income from shops and restaurants, accounts for 27.6 percent, donations make up 36.5 percent, and investment income from endowments accounts for 11.5 percent. As discussed in Chapter 3, there is no limit to the amount of money a nonprofit can make; what distinguishes a nonprofit institution is how that money is used. Their nonprofit status means that most museums exist as part of the public trust and therefore have legal and ethical responsibilities to the population they serve through their missions to collect, preserve, educate, and interpret objects. In other words, most museums in the United States are not fully supported by government funds, but are bound by law and duty to care for the collections they hold, preserve, and interpret to that public.

It requires a lot of money and many hours of labor to care for, interpret, and make accessible collections, and even more for a museum to be a dynamic institution. The traditional funding model for museums, a mix of entrance fees, memberships, donations, and some government funding, has proven to be inadequate and has already led to the unfortunate decline and even closing of some museums. Museum staff in the future will have to better understand their audiences, find new ways to bring in funds necessary for operations, and streamline how they go about their business. For example, most museums are open to the public between 9:00 a.m. and 5:00 p.m. on weekdays, despite the fact that most people in the United States live in two-income households and are thus unable to visit museums during those hours. Museums should consider opening after regular working hours as well as on weekends, when many people have leisure time to spend outside the home.

Although many museums have developed marketing strategies such as selling themed objects in their gift shops and online or renting out galleries and other spaces for special events, museums of the future will need to be more creative about funding. The ratio of collection size to staff size has grown increasingly skewed in museums due to budget constraints that limit the number of full-time staff positions, which require significant resources. In the future, better ways for fewer people to manage larger collections must be developed, such as using better collections management databases and applying a preventive conservation approach to collections care, as suggested by Simmons (2013).

Chapter 1 introduced the convergence movement that is currently growing among libraries, archives, and museums (LAM). Many futurists predict that convergence of these memory institutions will increase in the future, helping museums become more sustainable. At its core, the goal of LAM convergence is to create a system that will allow access to information across all collections in a unified digital system and in some cases, in a single physical location. This spirit of collaboration is driven by the desire to create a fuller, more comprehensive experience for users of these institutions. Convergence could lead to a new information environment, vastly more comprehensive than the current situation in which libraries, archives, and museums are separate institutional elements. While physical convergence may be problematic for many institutions, digital convergence is far more likely to take place, increasing access to collections. Convergence in its simplest form is the provision of access; access is the ability to have a resource not only available, but also consistently retrievable.

Trant notes that "the very idea of convergence arises from the fact that libraries, archives, and museums operate within common social, organizational, political, economic, and legal contexts" (2009, 378). It therefore stands to reason that convergence of LAM will allow institutions to capitalize on their commonalities in order to provide better services and access to users. Convergence will increase cost effectiveness and operational efficiency by removing the redundancies of separate institutions. By identifying the user needs addressed by each institution and incorporating the best parts of each of these institutions' services, a fully converged LAM institution could operate more efficiently and address user needs across the entire LAM spectrum. Whether or not this is the direction in which museums will evolve in the future is still being debated.

Shifting Demographics and Museum Audiences

Demographic shifts already underway will shape museums in the future. In 2010 the Center for the Future of Museums (of the American Alliance of Museums) produced a report on demographic shifts in the United States and how these changes will affect museum visitors and the way they visit institutions (Farrell and Medvedeva 2010). The report pointed out that the population of the United States is in the midst of major demographic changes. Today, minorities (defined as African American, Asian or Pacific Islander, American Indian, Alaska Native, and Hispanic or Latino) make up 34 percent of the U.S. population. In twenty-five years the population of the country will be 46 percent minority and well on its way to becoming minority majority not long after. Museums are clearly not doing enough now to attract minorities, when only 9 percent of the core visitors to museums are minorities. They must do much more in the future. Both museum visitors and the museum workforce should be representative of the population as a whole if museums of the future are to continue to be successful institutions. In addition to a growing minority population, the report addressed the fact that the children of immigrants are not the same as their parents, meaning that the generations born of immigrant parents will have expectations of museums that are different from the generation that came before them. In addition to these changes, museums must recognize that one in eight Americans is age sixty-five or older, but in twenty-five years, one in five will be. This means that in twenty-five years the overall population will have more older adults than it has now, another audience that museums will need to focus on and serve better.

Globalization and Localization

Museums will have to find ways to better serve their local communities while they operate in an increasingly global context. Access to the Internet and other communication technologies means that any museum, no matter how small or how isolated, can be a player on the world stage; yet at the same time, it is vitally important for museums to understand and serve the local communities that support them. As discussed in Chapter 9, museums have evolved in different ways in different parts of the world, yet they are still museums, still the places where objects and people meet.

Conclusion

Museums, like other nonprofit institutions, have to balance traditional practices with shifts in society. As has been discussed throughout this book, the problems facing museums today include declining funding coupled with increasing expenses; collection growth along with a reduction in collections care resources; digitization and its effects on access to objects and information; increasingly complicated policy and regulatory issues; the need to become more socially responsible; finding better ways to connect objects with the people who come to see them (visitors' interests vs. the curator's interests of the past); and the globalization of communities. In addition, museums must respond to the pressure on all nonprofit institutions to be more fully self-supporting. The future will bring greater expectations for open and transparent museum operations. Rapidly developing technologies mean that museums must make larger investments in both technology and staff training. Museums are also facing fluctuating attendance as well as changes in the number and roles of volunteers (AAM estimates that volunteers currently perform three times as much labor in museums as the paid staff, yet volunteer numbers are declining). Perhaps most important, museums must find ways to attract the best and the brightest young professionals and offer them a working environment that provides adequate compensation for their labor and opportunities for professional development.

The future of museums boils down to this: value. Will museums be valued in society? Will the citizens of a community, a city, a state, or a country consider museums to be so vital that if they disappear, something fundamental to their culture would be missing? How can museums with limited funds continue to thrive in an increasingly expensive world, yet continue to properly care for and communicate effectively the important heritage of the world? Museums must find ways to better and more cost effectively communicate what they do in order for the public to perceive their value to society. The only way for museums to stay relevant, for museum professionals to find funding and keep the public interested, is for the value of museums to be integrated into the very fabric of society. To do this will require persistent education on the part of those working in museums. Museum personnel need to continually and constantly teach the uniqueness of what they are doing and the importance of preserving the knowledge that is kept with physical collections. This means being vocal in local communities, using outreach to explain what museums do, and introducing children at a very young age to the ways of museum work and the importance of object knowledge and informal learning. This means that all museum workers, not just the directors or the public relations people, must constantly make an effort to spread the good word about museums. It is the *perception* of value that will help sustain museums in the future.

The issue of relevance should be a high priority in daily museum operations. Understanding how museum users value museums stems from an understanding of what museums mean, what their purpose is in society, and how they fit into the complicated systems of funding. These issues may sound grand and out of reach, but they are born in the daily work and decisions each museum worker makes.

Every member of the museum staff, including volunteers, plays a part in the perception of their museum. Every visitor's experience in the museum contributes to the perception of that museum. Elaine Gurian (2007) expressed this idea succinctly by saying that museums should strive to become essential rather than simply useful. Users should be free to explore their interests rather than being driven by organized presentations "by those in control" (museum workers). Gurian thinks that museums should be transformed from sites of occasional visits to become regular, essential, and daily parts of the average citizen's life.

The museum of tomorrow can continue to evolve in positive directions, changing from being useful to becoming essential to its users by focusing on understanding the way people and objects intersect in the museum system and beyond.

References

American Association of Museums. 1994. *Museums Count: A Report by the American Association of Museums*. Washington, DC: American Association of Museums.

Bell, Ford W. 2012. *How Are Museums Supported Financially in the United States?* Washington, DC: United States Department of State Bureau of International Information Programs.

Bell, Joshua A. 2012. "Museums as Relational Entities: The Politics and Poetics of Heritage." *Reviews in Anthropology* 41, no. 1: 70–90.

Duff, W. M., and J. M. Cherry. 2000. "Use of Historical Documents in a Digital World: Comparisons with Original Materials and Microfiche." *Information Research* 6, no. 1.

Farrell, B., and M. Medvedeva. 2010. *Demographic Transformation and the Future of Museums*. Washington DC: American Alliance of Museums Center for the Future of Museums.

Gosden, Chris, Francis Larson, and Alison Petch. 2007. *Knowing Things: Exploring the Collections at the Pitt Rivers Museum, 1884–1945*. London: Oxford University Press.

Gurian, Elaine H. 2007. "The Potential of Museum Learning: The Essential Museum," in *Manual of Museum Learning*, edited by Barry Lord, 21–41. Walnut Creek, CA: Altamira Press.

Hodder, Ian. 2012. *Entangled: An Archaeology of the Relationships between Humans and Things*. Malden, MA: Wiley-Blackwell.

Hooper-Greenhill, Eilean. 2000. "Changing Values in the Art Museum: Rethinking Communication and Learning." *International Journal of Heritage Studies* 6, no. 1: 9–31.

Latham, Kiersten F. n.d. Project Real Thing.

MacGregor, Neal. 2010. *A History of the World in 100 Objects*. New York: Viking.

Marty, Paul F. 2007. "Museum Websites and Museum Visitors: Before and After the Museum Visit." *Museum Management and Curatorship* 22, no. 4: 337–360.

Reach Advisors. 2010. "Museum Audience Insight." April 15, 21, 23. http://reach advisors.typepad.com.

Simmons, John E. 2013. "Application of Preventive Conservation to Solve the Coming Crisis in Collections Management," *Collection Forum* 27, nos. 1–2: 89–101.

Trant, Jennifer. 2009. "Emerging Convergence? Thoughts on Museums, Archives, Libraries, and Professional Training." *Museum Management and Curatorship* 24, no. 4: 369–387.

Index

About the Authors

KIERSTEN F. LATHAM is assistant professor in the School of Library and Information Science at Kent State University, Kent, OH, where she has developed the museum studies specialization within the MLIS program. Latham has worked in a diverse array of museums over a 20-year period. Her published works center around the museum as a holistic institution, the meaning of objects in human life, and the lived experience of museum visitors.

JOHN E. SIMMONS is an international museum consultant and lecturer who has worked in museums for more than 40 years. He has published widely on the care of natural history collections, collections management, and policy development.

CPSIA information can be obtained
at www.ICGtesting.com
Printed in the USA
FSHW011443160720
71827FS